PHILADELPHIA, PENNSYLVANIA
CUSTOM HOUSE RECONSTRUCTION

(22 Dec. 1719–7 Jan. 1724)

William Taylor Easter II

HERITAGE BOOKS
2017

HERITAGE BOOKS

AN IMPRINT OF HERITAGE BOOKS, INC.

Books, CDs, and more—Worldwide

For our listing of thousands of titles see our website
at
www.HeritageBooks.com

Published 2017 by
HERITAGE BOOKS, INC.
Publishing Division
5810 Ruatan Street
Berwyn Heights, Md. 20740

International Standard Book Numbers
Paperbound: 978-0-7884-5762-3

Contents

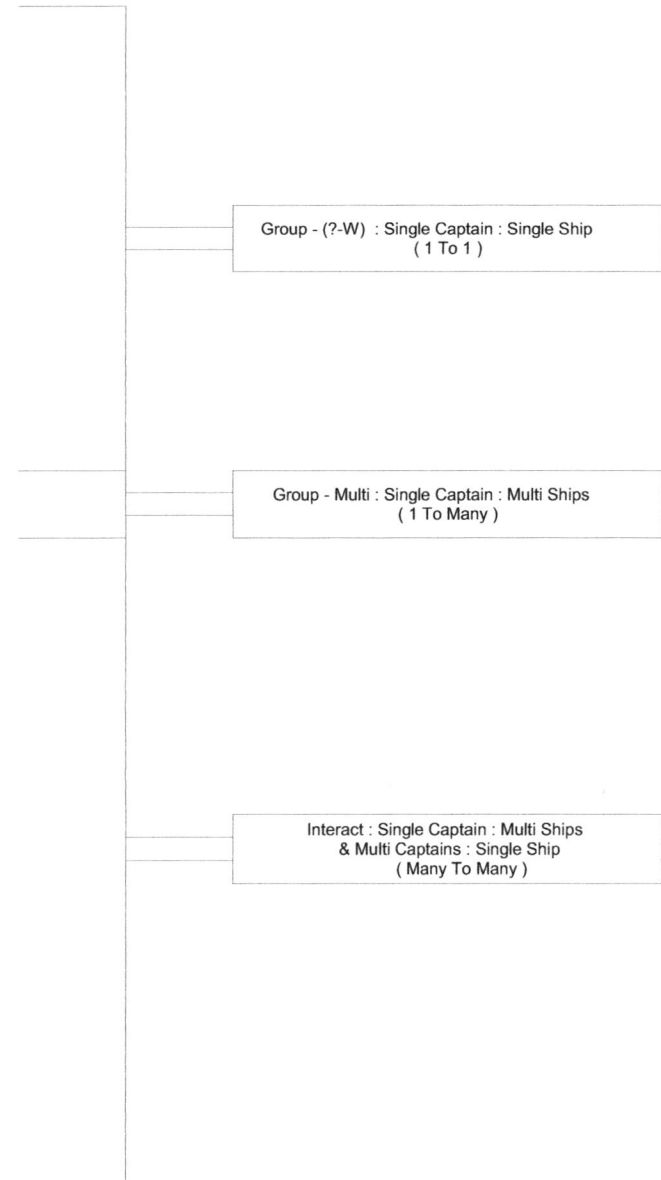

Group - (?-W) : Single Captain : Single Ship
(1 To 1)

Group - Multi : Single Captain : Multi Ships
(1 To Many)

Interact : Single Captain : Multi Ships
& Multi Captains : Single Ship
(Many To Many)

In genealogy we all know we are working on a puzzle that has no picture. When we look at the data, it is only a piece at a time, one date, one place, and one person. We can not get a whole grasp of what is going on. Think of a mosaic photo, if you look at it close up you see one small photo, but it is not what the overall photo looks like, if you take a few steps back it all comes into focus. That is what I have done with this book. I have tried to give you a picture for all the puzzle pieces that are between December 22,1719 – January 7,1724 for the Port of Philadelphia. You will see that getting a complete list of ships and their travels is the start of building a complete set of passenager records for this time period. More data is available for this time period than people think there is.Throughout the preface, I will explain how this data is laid out.

This is one of the first books for reconstructing a nearly complete list of ships and there voyages across the Atlantic and West Indies to and from Philadelphia. The data in this book was originally intended for the purpose of just reconstructing the records for the Custom House of just Philadelphia. But it had a different outcome when it was completed. It showed complete Arrival and Departure records for ships for years in a row to other ports besides Philadelphia. It shows interactions between ships and captains that previously were not known about.

This list started out with around 1453 captains with 1453 ships listed for those captains. After cross-referencing names,ships,ship types, dates, and ports; the list was combined down to 294 captains and 288 ships and the following is what that could not be validated as the same captains or ships. Two rules were followed:

Once you start looking over all the Arrival and Departure dates, you will start seeing how captains traded off with other captains. You will see how captains selected their own preferred routes .

I have covered the dates of December 22,1719 – January 7,1724. In total there was 1483 days. Out of the sources I used, only 49 days were not covered, which gives a 96.7% coverage for the Philadelphia Custom House. If you look at Preface X in this book you will see the coverage for the Custom House. You will see the missing data is in 7 day sections. So Arrival, Entered Out, Cleared Out, did not happen all in the same 7 days span, so in turn, you end up getting at least 2 out of the 3 events that happened for a ship. I will explain this on the following pages. So in the given time span you end up getting all captains and ships that interacted with the Philadelphia Custom House. Lets go a step farther and look at the partial data from captains and ships. In total there were 294 captains and 288 ships that interacted with the Custom House in the given date range. There were 7 partial captains, which means some data was missing from giving a 100% identification on those people, and there were 18 partial ships. So you have 94.22% coverage on captains, and 93.75% coverage on ships. So lets add all this into account when giving a more detailed coverage %... When you take all three sections into account you have a 94.89% coverage for the given date range.

Rule 1 – Assume all captains / masters with the same name are the same captain / unless ship name and ship type and / or arrival & departure dates comfirm otherwise.

Out of the 294 Captains 17 shared the same names, that is 5.78% of the total number.
It was not 5.78% of the same name; it was split up over 17 captains, the following is the breakdown of that list. Reasons for not combining are listed.

Matching Captains Names:

Bartlett, John - 3 / Elasped Time
Bird, Robert - 2 / Elasped Time
Hopkins, John - 2 / Elasped Time
Lindsey, David - 2 / Elasped Time
Richards, John - 2 / Elasped Time
Read, John - 2 / Elasped Time
Parker, Joseph - 2 / Elasped Time
Phillips, Matthew - 2 / Elasped Time

Odds are high that these captains do match, just the data was not there for 100% validation.

There was no conflicting data to state that they could not be conbined as the same person.

Legend: Reason for not combining

Elasped Time – Time between two ships with the same ports could be too short or too long to be compaired as the same ship.

Conflicting Dates & Ports – Two ships are at the same port at the same time or different ports are the same time.

Rule 2 – Assume all ships with same name and ship type are the same ship / unless captain name and / or arrival & departure dates confirm otherwise.

Out of the 288 Ships only 92 shared both names & types, that is 31.94% of the total number.
It was not 31.94% of the same ship; it was split up over 92 ships, the following is the breakdown of that list. Reasons for not combining are listed.

Matching Ship Name & Types:

Abigail / Brigantine – 2 / Elasped Time
Anne / Sloop – 4 / Elasped Time / Conflicting Dates & Ports
Benjamin / Sloop – 2 / Elasped Time
Carpenter / Sloop – 2 / Elasped Time
Charles / Sloop – 2 / Conflicting Dates & Ports
Deborah / Sloop – 2 / Conflicting Dates & Ports
Dolphin / Sloop – 5 / Conflicting Dates & Ports
Elizabeth / Sloop – 3 / Conflicting Dates & Ports
Endeavor / Sloop – 4 / Elasped Time / Conflicting Dates & Ports
Fancy / Sloop – 2 / Elasped Time
Hannah / Sloop – 2 / Elasped Time
Henry / Sloop – 2 / Conflicting Dates & Ports
Jane / Sloop – 3 / Elasped Time / Conflicting Dates & Ports
Margaret / Sloop – 3 / Conflicting Dates & Ports
Mary / Sloop – 8 / Elasped Time / Conflicting Dates & Ports
Mary Hope / Sloop – 2 / Elasped Time
Mayflower / Schooner – 2 / Elasped Time
Neptune / Sloop – 2 / Elasped Time / Conflicting Dates & Ports
Newport / Sloop – 3 / Conflicting Dates & Ports
Olive Branch / Sloop – 2 / Elasped Time
Philadelphia / Ship – 2 / Elasped Time
Sarah / Ship – 2 / Conflicting Dates & Ports
Sarah / Sloop – 4 / Conflicting Dates & Ports
Sarah & Mary / Sloop – 3 / Elasped Time / Conflicting Dates & Ports
Sea Flower / Sloop – 2 / Elasped Time
Speedwell / Sloop – 5 / Elasped Time / Conflicting Dates & Ports
Susanna / Sloop – 4 / Conflicting Dates & Ports
Three Brothers / Sloop – 2 / Conflicting Dates & Ports
Vine / Sloop – 2 / Elasped Time
William / Sloop – 7 / Elasped Time / Conflicting Dates & Ports

Odds are high that some of these ships do match, just the data was not there for 100% validation.

Preface

The following is a list of the totals of the years and how many captains and ships interacted with Phildelphia.

Total #		1720	1721	1722	1723
Captains: 294	Dates: 1453	Captains: 142	Captains: 116	Captains: 115	Captains: 99
Ships: 288	Ports: 1518	Ships: 130	Ships: 113	Ships: 102	Ships: 87

Known Arrivals – 1720				Known Arrivals – 1721				Known Arrivals – 1722				Known Arrivals – 1723			
Fortune	19 May 1720	Settlers	Many +	Nancy	14 Jun 1721	Settlers	Many +	Priscilla & Merriam	22 Aug 1722	Quaker	2 +	Faro	13 Jun 1723	Quaker	1 +
Laurel	30 Aug 1720	Palatine	340 +	Richard & Elizabeth	15 Sept 1721	Palatine	140 +	Hanover	3 Oct 1722	Palatine	130 +				
?	Nov 1720	Settlers	90 +	Little Anne	19 Oct 1721	Passenager	1 +	Globe	25 Oct 1722	Palatine	120 +				
?	27 Dec 1720	Workers	30 +					Pembroke	1 Nov 1722	Servants	30 +				
								Globe	Oct 1723	Palatine	1 +				
TOTAL: 460				TOTAL: 141				TOTAL: 283				TOTAL: 1			

Now you will see what each items means in the charts so you know how all the captains and ships interact.

Group	Ship				Captain / Master		Passage	Arrival / Departure 1		Passage	Arrival / Departure 2		Page
?	Year	Name	Type	Burden	First Name	Last Name	Length	Port	Arrival / Entered Inwards / Custom In / Entered Out	Length	Port	Arrival / Entered Inwards / Custom In / Entered Out	1
	MSTR ID#	Registry Location						State / Country	Custom Out / Cleared Out / Departure		State / Country	Custom Out / Cleared Out / Departure	
	SHIP ID#												
	Source							Notes					

Section: 1 / Group / Multi / Interact	
Group Multi Interact	These 3 can show up in the first box to let you know what group they are in.

Section: 2 / Ship	
Year	The years covered by the current ship being looked at.
MSTR ID#	Captain / Master ID Number
SHIP ID#	Ship ID Number
Name	Name of Ship
Type	Type of Ship / Sloop, Scallop, Brigantine, etc...
Burden	Weight of Ship / 100 Ton, 120 Tons, etc...
Registry Location	If location is known where ship is registred.

Section: 2.5 / Source	
Source	Source number and page number to locate data in source.

Section: 3 / Captain / Master	
First Name Last Name	First name of captain Last name of captain

Section: 4 & 6 / Passage	
Passage	This will have the length of passage or a symbol to show connection to the next port.

Section: 5 & 7 / Arrival & Departure	
Port	This is to show what port was for arrival or departure.
State / Country	This is to show what state in Colonial America, or other country.
Arrival / Entered Inwards	Date or Week ship entered port.
Custom In / Entered Out	Date or Week ship entered customs to load or unload cargo.
Custom Out / Cleared Out	Date or Week ship cleared customs for departure.
Departure	Date or Week ship left port.

Section: 5.5 / Notes	
Notes	Any notes available for passengers or other important data.

Section: 8 / Page	
Page	Page number of current page.

The next section is the legend for the dates and passage section.

Dates	
[? ? 1700] [? Jan 1700]	If you see a date in [ ] with a ? for the day or month then only partial data was available for event.
[7 Jan 1700]	When you see a date in [ ] it is a Post Date, the event happened within the last 7 days. Example / 1 Jan – 7 Jan 1700
(14 Jan 1700)	When you see a date in ( ) it is a Double Post Date, the event happened within the last 14 days. Example / 1 Jan – 14 Jan 1700
XX [7 Jan 1700] XX	If you see dates in gray, that means it shows where the next captain continues with the ship. To show how the two captains interacted when one enters the port and the other takes over.
7 Jan 1700	Exact date of event known when only a date is shown.

Port Names	
Port Names	If you see a port that is wrttien as Philadelphia, [Pennsylvania], only the data not in [ ] was given in the source data. The [ ] data is based off of what was in the source.

Passage	
Days / Weeks	In the passage section you may see days or weeks for the voyage length.
>	Data was complete to show next arrival & departure port for ship.
[>]	Enough data was complete to calculate next arrival & departure port for ship.

The example to the right shows what [>] is used for. There is data that we know that is from the week of [22 Dec 1719] that ship cleared customs in Phildelphia, and was headed to Barbados. Then on 20 Apr 1720 the same ship entered Philadelphia from Salt Island, Jamaica.

So by looking at this small example, it also shows where the passage took 18 days to Barbados. On average it takes about a month in port to enter customs, clear customs and depart.

Start	Philadelphia			18 Days	Barbados	
	[Pennsylvania]	[22 Dec 1719]				
[>]	Salt Island			>	Philadelphia	20 Apr 1720 XXXXXXXXXXXXXXX
	[Jamaica]				[Pennsylvania]	XX [7 Jul 1720] XX XXXXXXXXXXXXXXX

We know from documented passages from Jamaica to Philadelphia the travel time on average is 35 days, you can look at preface page IX to see the average passage times. By looking at the example chart below you see it would caclulate out to this ship having 36 days to complete its trip back to Philadelphia.

Barbados	Arrival	9 Jan 1720**
Port Layover Delay – 1 Month		
Barbados	Departure	9 Feb 1720**
Passage		7 Days**
Jamaica	Arrival	16 Feb 1720**
Port Layover Delay – 1 Month		
Jamaica	Departure	16 Mar 1720**
Passage		36 Days**
Philadelphia	Arrival	20 Apr 1720

Start	Philadelphia			18 Days	Barbados	9 Jan 1720
	[Pennsylvania]	[22 Dec 1719]				9 Feb 1720
[>]	Salt Island	16 Feb 1720		>	Philadelphia	20 Apr 1720 XXXXXXXXXXXXXXX
	[Jamaica]	16 Mar 1720			[Pennsylvania]	XX [7 Jul 1720] XX XXXXXXXXXXXXXXX

** Calculated Dates

American Weekly Mercury: Issue 107 / 2 Jan 1722

Note 1: When a ship winters at a port, the port layover can increase to 3 to 5 months from December to April if they dock at Philadelphia. The reason is the ice that blocked the Delaware River during the 1700's was a lot greater than it is today.

Note 2: If a ship does not winter in Philadelphia, they will leave by December and go to the West Indies and return by April.

Philadelphia, Jan. 5

No Veffel has arrived fince our laft, our River being locked up with Ice.

No Veffel has either been Entered or Cleared out this Week.

The next two examples will explain how captains and ships interact and switching out captains to new ships.

Example 1 – Interact 3 / Page 46 / Brigantine, *Esther*

1723	Esther	Brigantine		William		Dunlop	Start	Philadelphia	[9 May 1723]	>	Newfoundland	Never Left For This Port With	M-A-009
M-D-007									XX [27 Jun 1723] XX			This Ship	S-E-009
S-E-009								[Pennsylvania]	XXXXXXXXXXXXXXX				Page # 46
			8:50										

M-D-007		1723	Esther	Brigantine		John		Abbot	Start	Philadelphia	XXXXXXXXXXXXXXX	>	Newfoundland	
S-E-009	<	M-A-009									XX [9 May 1723] XX			
Page # 46		S-E-009								[Pennsylvania]	[27 Jun 1723]			
					8:70									

You can see from the example, that the Brigantine, *Esther* was in the following.

Philadelphia the week of 9 May 1723, Issue 177 of The *American Weekly Mercury*

Philadelphia the week of 27 Jun 1723, Issue 184 of The *American Weekly Mercury*

This is just a small example – Interact 3 / Page 46 only has 2 captains and 1 ship.

But the captains were different. The reason for this is, William Dunlop never left with the *Esther*. He stayed in Philadelphia and John Abbot took over the role as captain, then took the ship to Newfoundland. If you only look at the first entry in Issue 177 you only would think that William Dunlop was captain, and that he did take the ship to Newfoundland and you would be looking for the wrong captain if you needed to trace records. Seven Issues later, if you even would see it in the massive amount of data that the captain ended up changing, you may just think that there was just another ship going to the same place but in fact they were the same ship.

1723	Esther	Brigantine		William		Dunlop	Start	Philadelphia	[9 May 1723]	>	Newfoundland	Never Left For This Port With	M-A-009
M-D-007									XX [27 Jun 1723] XX			This Ship	S-E-009
S-E-009								[Pennsylvania]	XXXXXXXXXXXXXXX				Page # 46
			8:50										

M-D-007		1723	Esther	Brigantine		John		Abbot	Start	Philadelphia	XXXXXXXXXXXXXXX	>	Newfoundland	
S-E-009	<	M-A-009									XX [9 May 1723] XX			
Page # 46		S-E-009								[Pennsylvania]	[27 Jun 1723]			
					8:70									

Black Circles – When you see a box on the end of a ship with a Master ID & Ship ID – it matches the next captain that took over the role as captain on that ship.

Gray Circles – When you see a box on the front of a ship with a Master ID & Ship ID – it matches the previous captain of that ship.

Example 2 -Chart of Interact 27
Page 73 – 79

Solid Line: Connections Between
Ships that are the Same Ship

Dotted Line: Connections Between
Captains that are the Same Person

Interact 27 – Has 15 Captains & 14
Ships, Data came from 100 different
data entry's across 4 years of
newspapers

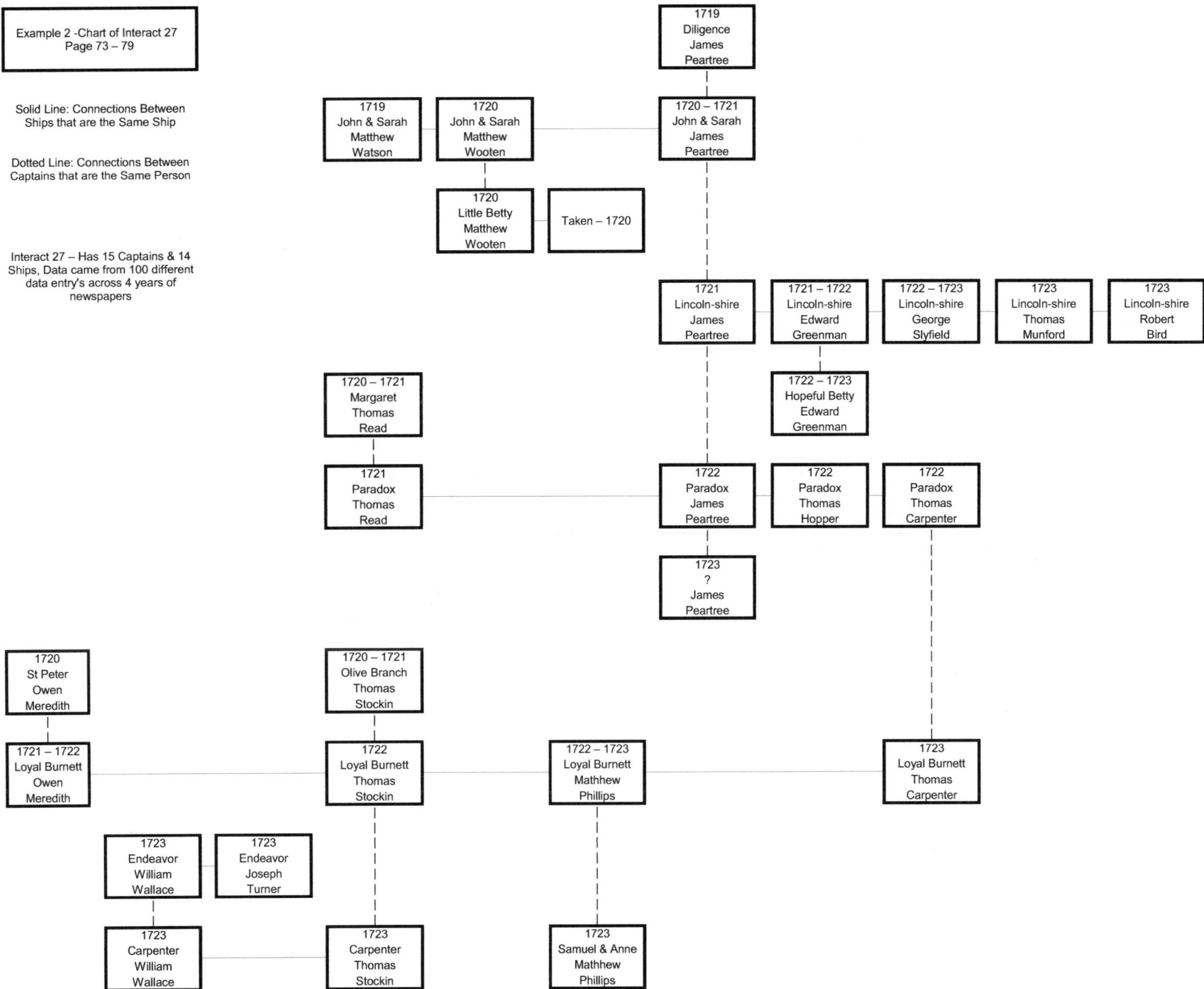

1719 Diligence James Peartree

| 1719 John & Sarah Matthew Watson | 1720 John & Sarah Matthew Wooten | 1720 – 1721 John & Sarah James Peartree |

| 1720 Little Betty Matthew Wooten | Taken – 1720 |

| 1721 Lincoln-shire James Peartree | 1721 – 1722 Lincoln-shire Edward Greenman | 1722 – 1723 Lincoln-shire George Slyfield | 1723 Lincoln-shire Thomas Munford | 1723 Lincoln-shire Robert Bird |

| 1722 – 1723 Hopeful Betty Edward Greenman |

| 1720 – 1721 Margaret Thomas Read |

| 1721 Paradox Thomas Read | 1722 Paradox James Peartree | 1722 Paradox Thomas Hopper | 1722 Paradox Thomas Carpenter |

| 1723 ? James Peartree |

| 1720 St Peter Owen Meredith |

| 1720 – 1721 Olive Branch Thomas Stockin |

| 1721 – 1722 Loyal Burnett Owen Meredith | 1722 Loyal Burnett Thomas Stockin | 1722 – 1723 Loyal Burnett Mathhew Phillips | 1723 Loyal Burnett Thomas Carpenter |

| 1723 Endeavor William Wallace | 1723 Endeavor Joseph Turner |

| 1723 Carpenter William Wallace | 1723 Carpenter Thomas Stockin | 1723 Samuel & Anne Mathhew Phillips |

This is an example of how this book can be used to track down how your ancestor came to Colonial America.

Extract out of the book " *Quaker Arrivals at Philadelphia 1682 – 1750* (Copyright 1902) " Page 76

These dates are Quaker dates so we have to convert them.

	Date	Place
Signed	18 Sept 1722	Pardshaw, England
Received	28 Jun 1723	Philadelphia, Pennsylvania

Certificate of Removal

JOHN STAMPER, a young man, dated 7 mo. 18, 1722, from Mo. Mtg. at Pardshaw Cragg, Cumberland, England. He "hath come amongst friends for Severall years past." Original on file. Received 4 mo. 28, 1723.

Now we take Page 11 from this book and compare.

1723	Faro	Brigantine		Thomas	New	Start	Bristol			Philadelphia	[13 Jun 1723]
M-N-002							[England]		>	[Pennsylvania]	[4 Jul 1723]
S-F-001											
						>	Lisbon				
							[Portugal]				
		8:66,73									

Name	John	Stamper	** Calulated Dates

Certificate / Friends Meeting	Pardshaw	England	18 Sept 1722
Travel / John Stamper			5 Months **
Location / John Stamper	Bristol	England	Feb 1723 **
Arrival / Brigantine – Faro	Bristol	England	14 – 28 Feb 1723 **
Customs / Brigantine – Faro	Bristol	England	14 Feb – 28 March 1723 **
Departure / Brigantine – Faro	Bristol	England	14 – 28 March 1723 **
Passage / Brigatime – Faro			11 – 13 Weeks **
Arrival / Brigantine – Faro	Philadelphia	Pennsylvania	7 – 13 Jun 1723
Certificate / Friends Meeting	Philadelphia	Pennsylvania	28 Jun 1723

Now that we have a nearly complete 94.89%+ list of every ship that entered & docked at Philadelphia from 22 Dec 1719 to 7 Jan 1724, we can now start constructing a passenger list for every ship. Ships that we did not even know that had passengers are now coming to light.

This will not be able to be done if you do not start with getting a complete list of ships. Almost every book that has been written to date has focused on one date, one place, one person at a time. You have to start from the ship and work your way down to the single person. Now every document that you find can be compared against a complete list of ships.

This is a example on how this book can be used to track down how your ancestor came to Colonial America.

Extract out of the book " *Quaker Arrivals at Philadelphia 1682 – 1750* (Copyright 1902) " Page 77-78
Also see book " *Immigration of the Irish Quakers into Pennsylvania 1682 – 1750* (Copyright 1902) " Page 291

These dates are Quaker dates so we have to convert them.

	Date	Place
Signed	23 Apr 1722	Cork, Ireland
Received	31 Aug 1722	Philadelphia, Pennsylvania

Now we take Page 29 from this book and compare.

Certificate of Removal

GEORGE and ELIZABETH DEEBLE, children of Richard Deeble, of Cork, deceased. The father died "about three years and a halfe [ago] and Left nine small children behinde him, over whom ye care of friends of this Citty for theire good has not been wanting and Some of theire near Relations in Pensilvania having Lately given Some Encouragement to Receive Some of them if they were Sent thither, the above named George and Eliza-beth ye two Eldest were very Desirous to go with a younger Sister." Dated 2 mo. 23, 1722, from Mtg. at Cork, Ireland. Received 6 mo. 31, 1722. Original on file.

1720 – 1723	Priscilla & Merriam	Ship										Philadelphia	18 Sept 1720 [31 Jan 1721]
M-R-008			John	Richards	Start	Barbados			>			[Pennsylvania]	[21 Feb 1721]
S-P-011													
					>	Barbados		[>]				Milford Haven	
												[Wales]	
					>	Cork			>			Philadelphia	[23 Aug 1722] [30 Aug 1722]
						[Ireland]						[Pennsylvania]	[11 Dec 1722]
					>	London			>			Downs	
						[England]						[England]	
					>	Philadelphia	[4 Oct 1723]						
						[Pennsylvania]							
5:103 / 6:14,20 / 7:99,102,142 / 8:106													

Name	George	Deeble
	Elizabeth	Deeble

** Caluclated Dates

As you can see from the last two example, you will now be able to see how your ancestor and the ship that they boarded reached the Philadelphia Custom House.

Certificate / Friends Meeting	Cork	Ireland	23 Apr 1722
Departure / Ship – Priscilla & Merriam	Milford Haven	Wales	24 – 30 Apr 1722 **
Arrival / Ship – Priscilla & Merriam	Cork	Ireland	7 – 14 May 1722 **
Customs / Ship – Priscilla & Merriam	Cork	Ireland	7 May – 7 Jun 1722 **
Departure / Ship – Priscilla & Merriam	Cork	Ireland	1 – 7 Jun 1722 **
Passage / Ship – Priscilla & Merriam			11 Weeks **
Arrival / Ship – Priscilla & Merriam	Philadelphia	Pennsylvania	17 – 23 Aug 1722
Certificate / Friends Meeting	Philadelphia	Pennsylvania	31 Aug 1722

Known Arrival & Departure Ports of the 1720's

America -------- >>>>   Direct   <<<< -------- Europe

America -------- >>>>   <<<< -------- Europe

Central

America -------- >>>>   <<<< -------- Europe

<<<< -------- Central

Central -------- >>>>

North America

St Johns	Newfoundland
Placentia	Newfoundland
Quebec	Canada
Annapolis Royal	Nova Scotia
New England	
Winter Harbor	Maine
Cape Porpoise	Maine
Piscataqua River	
Portsmouth	New Hampshire
Boston	Massachusetts
Nantasket	Massachusetts
Cape Ann	Massachusetts
Newport	Rhode Island
Saybrook	Connecticut
Hartford	Connecticut
New London	Connecticut
New Haven	Connecticut
Albany	New York
New York	New York
Long Island	New York
Perth Amboy	New Jersey
Sandy Hook	New Jersey
Salem	New Jersey
Burlington	New Jersey
Cape May	New Jersey
Philadelphia	Pennsylvania
Upland / Chester	Pennsylvania
Delaware River	
New Castle	Delaware
Prime Hook	Delaware
Lewes	Delaware
Port Lewis	Delaware
Cape Henlopen	Delaware
Annapolis	Maryland
Wye River	Maryland
Patuxent	Maryland
Potomac	Maryland
Choptank	Maryland
Sinepuxent	Maryland
Capes of Virginia	
	Virginia
James River	Virginia
Accomack	Virginia
York River	Virginia
Lynnhaven Bay	Virginia
	North Carolina
Bath Town	North Carolina
	South Carolina
Charles Town	South Carolina
St Augustine	Florida

American Coasters

Europe

Great Britain	
Isle of May	Scotland
Glasgow	Scotland
Montrose	Scotland
Lisburn	Ireland
Belfast	Ireland
Cork	Ireland
Londonderry	Ireland
Swansea	Wales
Milford Haven	Wales
Hull	England
Whitehaven	England
Torbay / Torquay	England
Plymouth	England
Exeter / Topsham	England
Cowes	England
Dartmouth	England
Dover	England
Deal	England
Bristol	England
London	England
Falmouth	England
Liverpool	England
Dolyserne	England
Sussex	England
Southampton	England
Isle of Wight	England
English Channel	
Rotterdam	Holland
	Holland
Bilbao	Spain
Santa Cruz	Spain
Oporto / Porto	Portugal
Lisbon	Portugal
Faial Island	Portugal
Madeira Island	Portugal

Europe Coasters

West Indies / South America

West Indies																				South America			
Bermuda	Bahamas	Bahamas	Bahamas	Barbados	Turks Islands	Montserrat	Virgin Islands	Antigua	Jamaica	Jamaica	Jamaica		Martinique	Providence		St Kitts & Nevis	St Christopher's			Leeward Islands	Canary Islands	Bay of Campeche	Campeche	Gulf of Honduras	Curacao	Suriname
	Walker Cay	Crooked Island					St Thomas		Spanish Town	Port Royal	Salt Island	St Martin						Nevis	Anguilla							

Average Passage Length & Ship Type / Sizes

Departure – North America

Charles Town	South Carolina	10 Days	Philadelphia	Pennsylvania
	North Carolina	18 Days	Perth Amboy	New Jersey
	Virginia	2 Days	Philadelphia	Pennsylvania
Philadelphia	Pennsylvania	18 Days	Barbados	
Philadelphia	Pennsylvania	7 Days	Bermuda	
Philadelphia	Pennsylvania	35 Days	London	England

Departure – West Indies & South America

Providence	14 Days	New York	New York
Providence	25 Days	New York	New York
Barbados	30 Days	Hartford	Connecticut
Barbados	21 Days	New York	New York
Barbados	22 Days	New York	New York
Barbados	22 Days	Perth Amboy	New Jersey
Barbados	18 Days		Rhode Island
Barbados	16 Days	Philadelphia	Pennsylvania
Jamaica	5 Weeks	Boston	Massachusetts
Jamaica	25 Days	New York	New York
Jamaica	28 Days	New York	New York
Jamaica	35 Days	New York	New York
Jamaica	35 Days	Philadelphia	Pennsylvania
Bermuda	28 Days	New York	New York
Bermuda	16 Days	Philadelphia	Pennsylvania
Curacao	17 Days	New York	New York
Curacao	19 Days	New York	New York
Curacao	21 Days	New York	New York
Curacao	26 Days	New York	New York
St Thomas	17 Days	New York	New York
St Thomas	20 Days	New York	New York

Departure – Europe

Cork	Ireland	10 Weeks	New York	New York
	Great Britain	10 Weeks	New York	New York
	Holland	11 Weeks	New York	New York
Downs	England	7 Weeks & 3 Days	New York	New York
Plymouth	England	6 Weeks	Piscataqua River	
Plymouth	England	7 Weeks	Philadelphia	Pennsylvania
Plymouth	England	9 Weeks	Philadelphia	Pennsylvania
Bristol	England	11 Weeks & 3 day	Philadelphia	Pennsylvania
Bristol	England	13 Weeks	Philadelphia	Pennsylvania
Madeira Island	Portugal	5 Weeks	New York	New York
Madeira Island	Portugal	6 Weeks & 5 Days	New York	New York
Swansea	Wales	15 Weeks	New York	New York
Exeter / Topsham	England	9 Weeks	Philadelphia	Pennsylvania
London	England	11 Weeks	Philadelphia	Pennsylvania
London	England	10 Weeks	New York	New York

Ship Types

Sloop	Tons: 3, 8,10,15, 22, 30, 32, 55
Ship	Tons: 100,130,150, 200, 240
Schooner	N / A
Scallop	N / A
Snow	N / A
Brigantine	N / A

X

Philadelphia, Pennsylvania	1719 – 1724
Data Coverage – Custom House – Weekly Post	

Legend

///	Data May Be Available For Week
X	Complete Data Available For Week
*	Dates Were Printed Wrong
Iss #	Issue Of Newspaper

The *American Weekly Mercury*	22 Dec 1719 – 7 Jan 1724
Issue 3: They did not publish any ship data, it was carried over into Issue 4.	

1719 - 6%

			Iss - #
////////	////////	///	
(rows of //////// //////// /// continue)			
12-16	12-22	X	1
12-23	12-29	X	2
No	Data		3

1720 – 94.3%

			Iss - #
12-30	1-8	X	4
////////	////////	///	5
1-16	1-25	X	6
1-26	2-2	X	7
////////	////////	///	8
2-10	2-16	X	9
2-17	2-23	X	10
2-24	3-1	X	11
3-2	3-7	X	12
No Date		X	13
////////	////////	///	14
3-22	3-31	X	15
4-1	4-7	X	16
4-8	4-14	X	17
4-15	4-21	X	18
4-22	4-28	X	19
4-29	5-5	X	20
5-6	5-12	X	21
5-13	5-19	X	22
5-20	5-26	X	23
5-27	6-1	X	24
6-2	6-9	X	25
6-10	6-16	X	26
6-17	6-23	X	27
6-24	6-30	X	28
7-1	7-7	X	29
7-8	7-14	X	30
7-15	7-21	X	31
7-22	7-28	X	32
7-29	8-4	X	33
8-5	8-11	X	34
8-12	8-18	X	35
8-19	8-25	X	36
8-26	9-1	X	37
9-2	9-8	X	38
9-9	9-15	X	39
9-16	9-22	X	40
9-23	9-29	X	41
9-30	10-6	X	42
10-7	10-13	X	43
10-14	10-20	X	44
10-21	10-27	X	45
10-28	11-3	X	46
11-4	11-10	X	47
11-11	11-17	X	48
11-18	11-24	X	49
11-25	12-1	X	50
12-2	12-8	X	51
12-9	12-13	X	52
12-14	12-20	X	53
12-21	12-27	X	54
12-28	1-3	X	55

1721 – 100%

			Iss - #
1-4	1-10	X	56
1-11	1-17	X	57
1-18	1-24	X	58
1-25	1-31	X	59
2-1	2-7	X	60
2-8	2-14	X	61
2-15	2-21	X	62
2-22	3-2	X	63
3-3	3-9	X	64
3-10	3-16	X	65
3-17	3-23	X	66
3-24	3-30	X	67
3-31	4-6	X	68
4-7	4-13	X	69
4-14	4-20	X	70
4-21	4-27	X	71
4-28	5-4	X	72
5-5	5-11	X	73
5-12	5-18	X	74
5-19	5-25	X	75
5-26	6-1	X	76
6-2	6-8	X	77
6-9	6-15	X	78
6-16	6-21	X	79
6-22	6-29	X	80
6-30	7-6	X	81
7-7	7-13	X	82
7-14	7-20	X	83
7-21	7-27	X	84
7-28	8-3	X	85
8-4	8-10	X	86
8-11	8-17	X	87
8-18	8-24	X	88
8-25	8-31	X	89
9-1	9-7	X	90
9-8	9-14	X	91
9-15	9-21	X	92
9-22	9-28	X	93
9-29	10-5	X	94
10-6	10-12	X	95
10-13	10-19	X	96
10-20	10-26	X	97
10-27	11-2	X	98
11-3	11-9	X	99
11-10	11-16	X	100
11-17	11-23	X	101
11-24	11-30	X	102
12-1	12-7	X	103
12-8	12-12	X	104
12-13	12-19	X	105
12-20	12-26	X	106
12-27	1-2	X	107

1722 – 98.07%

			Iss - #
1-3	1-9	X	108
1-10	1-16	X	109
1-17	1-22	X	110
////////	////////	///	111
1-30	2-6	X	112
2-7	2-13	X	113
2-12	*2-20	///	114
2-21	2-27	X	115
2-28	3-2	X	116
3-3	3-10	X	117
3-11	3-15	X	118
3-16	3-22	X	119
3-23	3-29	X	120
3-30	4-5	X	121
4-6	4-12	X	122
4-13	4-19	X	123
4-20	4-26	X	124
4-27	5-3	X	125
5-4	5-10	X	126
5-11	5-17	X	127
5-18	5-24	X	128
5-25	5-31	X	129
6-1	6-7	X	130
6-8	6-14	X	131
6-15	6-21	X	132
6-22	6-28	X	133
6-29	7-5	X	134
7-6	7-12	X	135
7-13	7-19	X	136
7-20	7-26	X	137
7-27	8-2	X	138
8-3	8-9	X	139
8-10	8-16	X	140
8-17	8-23	X	141
8-24	*8-30	X	142
8-31	9-6	X	143
9-7	9-13	X	144
9-14	9-20	X	145
9-21	9-27	X	146
9-28	10-3	X	147
10-4	*10-10	X	148
10-11	10-18	X	149
10-19	10-25	X	150
10-26	11-1	X	151
11-2	11-8	X	152
11-9	11-15	X	153
11-16	11-23	X	154
11-24	11-29	X	155
11-30	12-11	X	156
12-12	12-18	X	157
12-19	12-26	X	158
12-27	1-1	X	159

1723 – 94.2%

			Iss - #
1-2	1-8	X	160
1-9	1-14	X	161
1-15	1-21	X	162
1-22	1-29	X	163
1-30	2-5	X	164
2-6	2-12	X	165
2-13	*2-19	X	166
2-20	2-26	X	167
2-27	*3-7	X	168
3-8	3-14	X	169
3-15	3-21	X	170
////////	////////	///	171
3-29	4-4	X	172
////////	////////	///	173
4-12	4-18	X	174
4-19	4-25	X	175
4-26	5-2	X	176
5-3	5-9	X	177
5-10	5-16	X	178
5-17	5-23	X	179
5-24	5-30	X	180
5-31	6-6	X	181
6-7	6-13	X	182
6-14	6-20	X	183
6-21	6-27	X	184
6-28	7-4	X	185
7-5	7-11	X	186
7-12	7-18	X	187
7-19	7-25	X	188
7-26	7-29	X	189
7-30	8-8	X	190
8-9	8-15	X	191
8-16	8-22	X	192
8-23	8-29	X	193
8-30	9-5	X	194
9-6	9-12	X	195
9-13	9-19	X	196
9-20	9-26	X	197
9-27	10-4	X	198
10-5	10-11	X	199
10-12	10-17	X	200
10-18	10-24	X	201
10-25	10-31	X	202
11-1	11-7	X	203
11-8	11-14	X	204
11-15	11-21	X	205
11-22	11-29	X	206
11-30	12-5	X	207
12-6	12-9	X	208
12-10	12-17	X	209
12-18	12-24	X	210
////////	////////	///	211

1724 – 1.9%

			Iss - #
1-1	*1-7	X	212
////////	////////	///	

Group	Ship				Captain / Master		Passage	Arrival / Departure 1		Passage	Arrival / Departure 2		Page
	Year	Name	Type	Burden	First Name	Last Name	Length	Port	Arrival / Entered Inwards / Custom In / Entered Out	Length	Port	Arrival / Entered Inwards / Custom In / Entered Out	
?	MSTR ID#	Registry Location						State / Country	Custom Out / Cleared Out / Departure		State / Country	Custom Out / Cleared Out / Departure	1
	SHIP ID#												
	Source							Notes					

1723		Sloop					Start	Antigua		>	Philadelphia	[4 Oct 1723]
M-?-001												
S-?-001											[Pennsylvania]	
8:106												

1722					John	Bartlett	Start	Boston		>		
M-B-001								[Massachusetts]	[8 Oct 1722]		Pennsylvania	
S-?-002												
20:62												

1723					John	Bartlett	Start	Boston		>	Philadelphia	
M-B-002								[Massachusetts]	[16 Mar 1723]		[Pennsylvania]	
S-?-003												
20:84												

1719						Hudson	Start	Philadelphia		>		
M-H-001								[Pennsylvania]	[22 Dec 1719]		Carolina	
S-?-004												
5:2												

1719 – 1720		Schooner				Thorp	Start	Philadelphia		>	Lisbon	Before 22 Nov 1719
M-T-001								[Pennsylvania]			[Portugal]	
S-?-005												
							[>]	Barbados		>	Capes of Virginia	Before 19 May 1720
												Taken / Spanish Privateer
							>		Never Reached Port			
								Virginia	Taken / Spanish Privateer			
5:22,53												

1720							Start	?		>	Herring Bay	Before 27 Dec 1720
M-?-002											Maryland	
S-?-006												
							[L]	Philadelphia				
								[Pennsylvania]				
6:4								(Known Passengers / Workers) Herring Bay / Inward – 27 Dec 1720 – Count 30+				
								Upon Account of the Hemp Manufacturer / Intended to be Settled in Philadelphia				

Group	Year	Name	Type	Burden	First Name	Last Name	Length	Port / State-Country	Arrival / Custom / Departure 1	Length	Port / State-Country	Arrival / Custom / Departure 2	Page
?													2

Group	Ship				Captain / Master		Passage	Arrival / Departure 1		Passage	Arrival / Departure 2		Page
	Year / MSTR ID# / SHIP ID# / Registry Location / Source	Name	Type	Burden	First Name	Last Name	Length	Port / State / Country	Arrival / Entered Inwards — Custom In / Entered Out — Custom Out / Cleared Out — Departure	Length	Port / State / Country	Arrival / Entered Inwards — Custom In / Entered Out — Custom Out / Cleared Out — Departure	

Year / IDs	Type	First Name	Last Name	Length	Port 1 / State	Dates 1	Length	Port 2 / State	Dates 2
1719 – 1720 / M-R-001 / S-?-007	Sloop	Bartholomew	Radford	Start	Philadelphia [Pennsylvania]	[22 Dec 1719]	>	Suriname	
				>	Virginia	21 Jun 1720	>	Cape Henlopen [Delaware]	23 Jun 1720
				>	Philadelphia [Pennsylvania]	26 Jun 1720			
Source: 5:2,70									
1723 / M-J-001 / S-?-008		Thomas	Jenkins	Start	Pennsylvania		>	Boston [Massachusetts]	[17 Aug 1723]
Source: 20:107									
1723 / M-P-001 / S-?-009		Jacob	Philips	Start	Boston [Massachusetts]	[4 May 1723] / [11 May 1723]	>	Pennsylvania	
Source: 20:92,93									
1720 / M-B-003 / S-?-010	Brigantine		Bailey	Start	?		>	Philadelphia [Pennsylvania]	Never Reached Port / Taken / Spanish Privateer
				>	St Thomas / Virgin Islands	Before [28 Jul 1720] / Carried Into This Port			
Source: 5:78,82									
1723 / M-B-004 / S-?-011			Butterfield	Start	Bermuda		16 Days	Philadelphia [Pennsylvania]	18 Apr 1723
Source: 8:39									
1720 / M-?-003 / S-?-012	Brigantine			Start	Londonderry [Ireland]		>	Delaware Bay	27 Oct 1720
				>	Philadelphia [Pennsylvania]				
Source: 5:120									

Notes: (Known Passengers / Settlers) Philadelphia / Inward – Nov 1720 – Count 90+

Group	Ship Year	Name	Type	Burden	MSTR ID# / SHIP ID#	Registry Location	First Name	Last Name	Passage Length	A/D 1 Port	State / Country	Arrival/Custom/Departure	Passage Length	A/D 2 Port	State / Country	Arrival/Custom/Departure	Page
A																	3
	1720	*Adventure*	Sloop		M-S-001 / S-A-001		Joseph	Smith	Start	Philadelphia	[Pennsylvania]	[7 Mar 1720] / [14 Mar 1720]	>	Barbados			
									[>]	Antigua			>	Philadelphia	[Pennsylvania]	[16 Jun 1720] / [23 Jun 1720] / [18 Aug 1720]	
									>	Barbados			[>]	St Christopher's			
									>	Philadelphia	[Pennsylvania]	24 Nov 1720 / [8 Dec 1720] / [27 Dec 1720]	>	Jamaica			

XXXXXXXXX XXXXXXXXX Captain / Master Changed Ships XXXXXXXXX XXXXXXXXX

Group	Year	Name	Type	Burden	MSTR ID# / SHIP ID#	First	Last	Passage	Port	State/Country	Dates	Passage	Port 2	Notes
	1722	*Anne*	Sloop		S-A-005			Start	Philadelphia	[Pennsylvania]	[26 Apr 1722] / XX [7 Jun 1722] XX / XXXXXXXXXXXXX	>	St Christopher's	Never Left For Port / See Next Ship Or Captain

XXXXXXXXX XXXXXXXXX Captain / Master Changed Ships XXXXXXXXX XXXXXXXXX

| | 1722 | *Margaret* | Sloop | | S-M-002 | | | Start | Philadelphia | [Pennsylvania] | XXXXXXXXXXXXX / XX [26 Apr 1722] XX / [7 Jun 1722] | > | St Christopher's | |
| | | | | | | | | > | Philadelphia | [Pennsylvania] | [10 Oct 1722] | | | |

5:24,27,63,67,90,133,138 / 6:4 / 7:46,48,68,118

| | 1722 – 1723 | *Adventure* | Brigantine | | M-A-001 / S-A-002 | William | Annis | Start | Philadelphia | [Pennsylvania] | [11 Dec 1722] | > | Jamaica | |
| | | | | | | | | [>] | Philadelphia | [Pennsylvania] | [2 May 1723] | > | Lisbon [Portugal] | |

7:142 / 8:46

| | 1720 | *Anne* | Sloop | | M-S-002 / S-A-004 | Samuel | Story | Start | | South Carolina | | > | Philadelphia [Pennsylvania] | [14 Jul 1720] / [21 Jul 1720] / [4 Aug 1720] |
| | | | | | | | | > | | South Carolina | | | | |

5:75,78,86

| | 1721 | *Anne* | Brigantine | | M-S-004 / S-A-006 | Edward | Smith | Start | Liverpool | [England] | | > | Philadelphia [Pennsylvania] | 24 Jun 1721 / [10 Aug 1721] / [12 Oct 1721] |
| | | | | | | | | > | Jamaica | | | | | |

6:67,90,115

Group	Ship				Captain / Master		Passage	Arrival / Departure 1		Passage	Arrival / Departure 2		Page
A – B	Year	Name	Type	Burden	First Name	Last Name	Length	Port	Arrival / Entered Inwards / Custom In / Entered Out / Custom Out / Cleared Out / Departure	Length	Port	Arrival / Entered Inwards / Custom In / Entered Out / Custom Out / Cleared Out / Departure	4
	MSTR ID# / SHIP ID#	Registry Location						State / Country			State / Country		
	Source							Notes					

Anne (1723)

- MSTR ID#: M-H-002
- SHIP ID#: S-A-007
- Type: Sloop
- Captain / Master: Robert Holmes

Passage	Arrival / Departure 1	Dates	Passage	Arrival / Departure 2	Dates
Start	New York [New York]	(1 Apr 1723)	>	Boston [Massachusetts]	[13 Apr 1723] / [4 May 1723]
>	Pennsylvania		>	Boston [Massachusetts]	[6 Jul 1723] / [13 Jul 1723]
>	Pennsylvania				

Source: 8:34 / 20:89,92,101,102

Bachelor (1720)

- MSTR ID#: M-W-001
- SHIP ID#: S-B-001
- Type: Sloop
- Captain / Master: Matthew Wilson

Passage	Arrival / Departure 1	Dates	Passage	Arrival / Departure 2
Start	Philadelphia [Pennsylvania]	[31 Mar 1720] / [14 Apr 1720]	>	Annapolis [Maryland]

Source: 5:32,36

Benjamin (1719 – 1721)

- MSTR ID#: M-G-002
- MSTR ID#: M-B-002
- Type: Sloop
- Captain / Master: Ephraim Gilbert

Passage	Arrival / Departure 1	Dates	Passage	Arrival / Departure 2	Dates
Start	Madeira Island [Portugal]	18 Nov 1719	>	Bermuda	Dec 1719 – Jan 1720
28 Days	New York [New York]	20 Feb 1720	[>]	Jamaica	
>	Philadelphia [Pennsylvania]	3 Oct 1720 / [27 Oct 1720]	>	Barbados	
[>]	Bermuda		>	Philadelphia [Pennsylvania]	[20 Apr 1721] / [27 Apr 1721] / [11 May 1721]
>	Jamaica				

Source: 5:24,110,120 / 6:40,42,46

Notes: (Ship) Bermuda / Infected Small Pox – Dec 1719

Benjamin (1720)

- MSTR ID#: M-N-001
- SHIP ID#: S-B-003
- Type: Schooner
- Captain / Master: Richard Newcomb

Passage	Arrival / Departure 1	Passage	Arrival / Departure 2	Dates
Start	Lewis Town [Delaware]	>	Philadelphia [Pennsylvania]	[12 May 1720]

Source: 5:50

Group	Year	Name	Type	Burden	First Name	Last Name	Length	Port / State/Country	Arr. Dep. 1 dates	Length	Port / State/Country	Arr. Dep. 2 dates	Page
B													5

B-005 / S-B-004
	1722	*Benjamin*	Sloop		Samuel	Burrows	Start	Jamaica		>	Philadelphia [Pennsylvania]	[16 Aug 1722] [30 Aug 1722] [20 Sept 1722]	
	M-B-005 / S-B-004						>	Jamaica					
	Source: 7:96,102,110												

S-B-005
	1721	*Benjamin*	Brigantine		Arthur	Payne	Start	Philadelphia [Pennsylvania]	[20 Jul 1721] [23 Nov 1721]	>	Madeira Island [Portugal]		
	M-P-002 / S-B-005												
	Source: 6:79,134												

S-B-006
	1722	*Benjamin & Mary*	Sloop		Robert	Hunter	Start	New Providence		>	Philadelphia [Pennsylvania]	[18 Oct 1722] [23 Nov 1722]	
	M-H-003 / S-B-006						>	North Carolina					
	Source: 7:120,136												

S-B-007
	1722	*Bersheba*	Sloop		Samuel	Fox	Start	Antigua		>	Philadelphia [Pennsylvania]	[2 Aug 1722] [9 Aug 1722] [20 Sept 1722]	
	M-F-002 / S-B-007						>	Barbados					
	Source: 7:92,94,110												

S-B-009
	1722	*Blessing*	Sloop		Joseph	Evans	Start	Turks Island		>	Philadelphia [Pennsylvania]	[9 Aug 1722] [16 Aug 1722] [6 Sept 1722]	
	M-E-001 / S-B-009						>	Jamaica					
	Source: 7:94,96,106												

S-B-010
	1721	*Boneta*	Brigantine		James	Murgatroyd	Start	Londonderry [Ireland]		>	Philadelphia [Pennsylvania]	9 Nov 1721 [30 Nov 1721] [7 Dec 1721]	
	M-M-001 / S-B-010						>	Madeira Island [Portugal]					
	Source: 6:130,138,140												

Group	Ship				Captain / Master		Passage	Arrival / Departure 1		Passage	Arrival / Departure 2		Page
	Year	Name	Type	Burden	First Name	Last Name	Length	Port	Arrival / Entered Inwards / Custom In / Entered Out	Length	Port	Arrival / Entered Inwards / Custom In / Entered Out	
B – C	MSTR ID#								Custom Out / Cleared Out			Custom Out / Cleared Out	6
	SHIP ID#	Registry Location						State / Country	Departure		State / Country	Departure	
	Source						Notes						

1723	*Britannia*	Brigantine			William	Mayberry / Maybury	Start			>	Philadelphia	[6 Jun 1723]	
M-M-002								South Carolina			[Pennsylvania]	[4 Jul 1723]	
S-B-011													
							>	Jamaica		>	Philadelphia	[14 Nov 1723] [29 Nov 1723]	
											[Pennsylvania]	[5 Dec 1723]	
							>	South Carolina					
	8:62,126,130												

1721	*Builders Adventure*	Sloop			Joseph	Toest	Start	St Christopher's		>	Philadelphia	1 Aug 1721	
M-T-002											[Pennsylvania]		
S-B-012		6:87											

1720 – 1721	*Charles*	Sloop			Joseph	Arthur	Start	Philadelphia	[1 Mar 1720]	>	Antigua		
M-A-002								[Pennsylvania]	[31 Mar 1720]				
S-C-003													
							>	Philadelphia	14 Jul 1720 [28 Jul 1720]	>	Antigua		
								[Pennsylvania]	[4 Aug 1720]				
							[>]	Anguilla		>	Philadelphia	23 Nov 1720 [8 Dec 1720]	
											[Pennsylvania]	[20 Dec 1720]	
							>	Antigua		>	Anguilla		
							>	Philadelphia	[4 Apr 1721] [4 May 1721]	>	Antigua		
								[Pennsylvania]	[1 Jun 1721]				
							>	Philadelphia	15 Sept 1721 [9 Nov 1721]	>	Antigua		
								[Pennsylvania]	[7 Dec 1721]				

XXXXXXXXX XXXXXXXXX Captain / Master Changed Ships XXXXXXXXX XXXXXXXXX

1723	*Clementine*	Brigantine					>	Philadelphia	[27 Jun 1723] [11 Jul 1723]	>	Antigua		
S-C-007								[Pennsylvania]					
							>	St John's	20 Sept 1723	>	St John's	Lost In Harbor / Hurricane	
								Antigua	Lost		Antigua		
	5:22,32,75,78,82,86,133,138 / 6:2,36,44,56,106,130,140 / 8:70,76,126												

Group	Year / MSTR ID# / SHIP ID#	Ship Name / Registry Location / Source	Type	Burden	First Name	Last Name	Passage Length	Arr/Dep 1 Port / State-Country	Arr/Dep 1 Dates	Passage Length	Arr/Dep 2 Port / State-Country	Arr/Dep 2 Dates
C	1720 / M-C-001 / S-C-002	Catherine	Ship		William	Car	Start	Londonderry [Ireland]		>	Philadelphia [Pennsylvania]	[9 Nov 1721] [16 Nov 1721]
							>	Glasgow [Scotland]				
	6:130,132											
C	1722 / M-G-004 / S-C-004	Charming Sally	Ship	200 Tons	James	Gruchy	Start	Philadelphia [Pennsylvania]	[19 Apr 1722] [25 Oct 1722]	>	London [England]	
	7:46,54,58,64,68,80,86,122											
C	1723 / M-R-002 / S-C-005	Charming Molly	Ship		John	Richards	Start	Philadelphia [Pennsylvania]	[9 Dec 1723]	>	Barbados	
	8:134											
C	1721 / M-B-006 / S-C-006	Clarendon Packet	Sloop		Elisha	Bennett	Start	New York [New York]	[5 Jun 1721] [19 Jun 1721]	>	Boston [Massachusetts]	
								New York [New York]	20 Jul 1721 [4 Sept 1721] [25 Sept 1721]	>	Boston [Massachusetts]	
							>	New York [New York]	[23 Nov 1721]	>	Philadelphia [Pennsylvania]	[7 Dec 1721] [7 Dec 1721] [19 Dec 1721]
							>	New York [New York]	(19 Dec 1721)			
	6:58,63,84,100,108,137,140,146,148											
C	1721 / M-H-004 / S-C-008	Cocoa Nut	Sloop		Lambert	Hilmont	Start	Jamaica		>	Philadelphia [Pennsylvania]	13 Jul 1721 [21 Sept 1721] [2 Nov 1721]
							>	Jamaica				
	6:79,106,125											
C	1722 / M-K-001 / S-C-009	Content	Sloop		William	Keele	Start	Bermuda		>	Philadelphia [Pennsylvania]	[26 Apr 1722] [10 May 1722] [24 May 1722]
							>	Jamaica				
	7:48,54,60											

Group	Year / MSTR ID# / SHIP ID#	Name	Type	Burden / Registry Location	First Name	Last Name	Passage Length	Port / State-Country (1)	Arrival / Entered Inwards · Custom In / Entered Out · Custom Out / Cleared Out · Departure (1)	Passage Length	Port / State-Country (2)	Arrival / Entered Inwards · Custom In / Entered Out · Custom Out / Cleared Out · Departure (2)	Source / Notes
	1722 / M-P-002 / S-C-010	*Cutwater*	Sloop		John	Price	Start	Bath Town / North Carolina		>	Philadelphia / [Pennsylvania]	[26 Apr 1722] / [3 May 1722] / [3 May 1722]	
							>	Lewes / [Delaware]					7:48,52
	1720 / M-S-005 / S-D-001	*Deborah*	Sloop			Sipkins	Start	/ Virginia		>	Bermuda	Never Reached Port / Taken / Spanish Privateer	
							>	Capes of Virginia	?? ??? 1720 / Taken / Spanish Privateer	>	?	?? ??? 1720 / Retaken / Spanish Privateer	
							>	Philadelphia / [Pennsylvania]	[10 Nov 1720]				5:126
	1722 / M-C-002 / S-D-002	*Digby*	Sloop		Thomas	Collins	Start	Jamaica		>	Philadelphia / [Pennsylvania]	[23 Aug 1722] / [11 Dec 1722]	
							>	Jamaica					7:99,142
	1723 / M-M-004 / S-D-003	*Dolphin*	Sloop		Isaac	Martindal	Start	/ Rhode Island		>	Philadelphia / [Pennsylvania]	[22 Aug 1723] / [22 Aug 1723] / [12 Sept 1723]	
							>	/ Rhode Island					8:91,98
	1720 / M-M-005 / S-D-004	*Dolphin*	Sloop		Edward	Maugier	Start	Philadelphia / [Pennsylvania]	[7 Jul 1720]	>	Antigua		5:72

Group	Year / MSTR ID# / SHIP ID#	Ship Name / Registry Location	Type	Burden	First Name	Last Name	Passage Length	Arrival/Departure 1 Port / State/Country	Arr 1 dates	Passage Length	Arrival/Departure 2 Port / State/Country	Arr 2 dates	Page
D – E													9

Ship 1 — Dorothy

- Year: 1720 – 1721
- MSTR ID#: M-B-007
- SHIP ID#: S-D-005
- Name: *Dorothy*, Type: Ship
- Captain/Master: William Bull

Passage Length	Arrival/Departure 1 Port [State/Country]	Dates	Passage Length	Arrival/Departure 2 Port [State/Country]	Dates
Start	Bristol [England]		>	11 Jun 1720 – Main Mast Split By Lightning / Violent Storm 50 Leagues from Cape Henlopen	
>	Sandy Hook [New Jersey]		>	Philadelphia [Pennsylvania]	5 Jul 1720 / [11 Aug 1720] / [18 Aug 1720]
>	Virginia		[>]	Bristol [England]	29 Aug or 4 Sept 1721
>	Philadelphia [Pennsylvania]	[23 Nov 1721] / [12 Dec 1721] / [29 Mar 1722]	>	Jamaica	

Source: 5:70,72,88,90 / 6:125,134,144 / 7:38

Ship 2 — Duck

- Year: 1723
- MSTR ID#: M-T-002
- SHIP ID#: S-D-006
- Name: *Duck*, Type: Sloop
- Captain/Master: Robert Townsend

Passage Length	Arrival/Departure 1 Port	Passage Length	Arrival/Departure 2 Port [State/Country]	Dates
Start	New Providence	>	Philadelphia [Pennsylvania]	[25 Apr 1723] / [2 May 1723] / [9 May 1723]
>	New Providence			

Source: 8:42,46,50

Ship 3 — Elizabeth

- Year: 1721
- MSTR ID#: M-B-008
- SHIP ID#: S-E-001
- Name: *Elizabeth*, Type: Sloop
- Captain/Master: William Brown

Passage Length	Arrival/Departure 1 Port	Passage Length	Arrival/Departure 2 Port [State/Country]	Dates
Start	Nevis	>	Philadelphia [Pennsylvania]	19 Jun 1721 / [29 Jun 1721] / [29 Jun 1721]
>	Rhode Island			

Source: 6:63,67

Ship 4 — Elizabeth

- Year: 1721
- MSTR ID#: M-M-006
- SHIP ID#: S-E-002
- Name: *Elizabeth*, Type: Sloop
- Captain/Master: Nathaniel Mariner

Passage Length	Arrival/Departure 1 Port	Passage Length	Arrival/Departure 2 Port [State/Country]	Dates
Start	South Carolina	>	Philadelphia [Pennsylvania]	10 Aug 1721 / [24 Aug 1721] / [7 Sept 1721]
>	South Carolina			

Source: 6:92,94,100

Ship 5 — Elizabeth & Anne

- Year: 1722
- MSTR ID#: M-T-002
- SHIP ID#: S-E-003
- Name: *Elizabeth & Anne*, Type: Sloop
- Captain/Master: John Tucker

Passage Length	Arrival/Departure 1 Port	Passage Length	Arrival/Departure 2 Port [State/Country]	Dates
Start	Turks Island	>	Philadelphia [Pennsylvania]	[12 Apr 1722] / [3 May 1722] / [7 Jun 1722]
>	Jamaica			

Source: 7:42,52,68

Group	Ship					Captain / Master		Passage	Arrival / Departure 1		Passage	Arrival / Departure 2		Page
	Year	Name	Type	Burden		First Name	Last Name	Length	Port	Arrival / Entered Inwards / Custom In / Entered Out	Length	Port	Arrival / Entered Inwards / Custom In / Entered Out	
E	MSTR ID#	Registry Location							State / Country	Custom Out / Cleared Out / Departure		State / Country	Custom Out / Cleared Out / Departure	10
	SHIP ID#													
	Source								Notes					

1720 – 1723	Elizabeth & Hannah	Sloop				Elias	Wair / Wiar	Start	Boston		>	Philadelphia	[1 Jun 1720] [1 Jun 1720] [23 Jun 1720]	
M-W-011									[Massachusetts]			[Pennsylvania]		
S-E-007														
								>	Boston		>	Philadelphia	16 Aug 1720 [25 Aug 1720] [8 Sept 1720]	
									[Massachusetts]			[Pennsylvania]		
								>	Boston	[10 Sept 1720]	>	Delaware River	17 Oct 1720	
									[Massachusetts]					
								>	Philadelphia	[27 Oct 1720] [10 Nov 1720]	>	Boston		
									[Pennsylvania]			[Massachusetts]		
								>	Philadelphia	12 Apr 1721 [27 Apr 1721] [11 May 1721]	>	Boston		
									[Pennsylvania]			[Massachusetts]		
								>	Philadelphia	8 Jul 1721 [20 Jul 1721] [27 Jul 1721]	>	Boston		
									[Pennsylvania]			[Massachusetts]		
								>	Philadelphia	[2 Nov 1721] [2 Nov 1721] [30 Nov 1721]	>	Boston	[14 May 1722] [28 May 1722]	
									[Pennsylvania]			[Massachusetts]		
								>	Philadelphia	[28 Jun 1722] [28 Jun 1722] [5 Jul 1722]	>	Boston	[23 Jul 1722] [8 Oct 1722]	
									[Pennsylvania]			[Massachusetts]		
								>	Philadelphia		>	Boston	[4 May 1723] [4 May 1723] [25 May 1723]	
									[Pennsylvania]			[Massachusetts]		
								>	Philadelphia		>	Boston	[17 Aug 1723] [24 Aug 1723] [7 Sept 1723]	
									[Pennsylvania]			[Massachusetts]		
								>	Newport		>	Perth Amboy		
									[Rhode Island]			[New Jersey]		
5:58,67,90,92,96,106,115,120,126 / 6:38,42,46,76,79,84,125,138 / 7:76,79 / 20:41,43,51,62,92,95,107,108,110														

Group	Year / MSTR ID# / SHIP ID#	Ship Name	Type	Burden	First Name	Last Name	Passage Length	Port / State-Country	Arrival/Departure 1	Passage Length	Port / State-Country	Arrival/Departure 2	Page
E – F													11

Elizabeth & Martha — Sloop
- Year: 1721
- MSTR ID#: M-G-005
- SHIP ID#: S-E-004
- Captain/Master: John Gibbs
- Passage 1: Start — Bermuda
- Arrival/Departure 2: Philadelphia [Pennsylvania] — 7 Aug 1721 / [24 Aug 1721] / [7 Sept 1721]
- > Barbados
- Source: 6:90,94,100

Endeavor — Sloop
- Year: 1720
- MSTR ID#: M-W-002
- SHIP ID#: S-E-005
- Captain/Master: Thomas Wright
- Passage 1: Start — St Christopher's
- Arrival/Departure 2: Philadelphia [Pennsylvania] — 26 Jul 1720 / [18 Aug 1720] / [1 Sept 1720]
- > St Christopher's
- Source: 5:82,90,94

Exchange — Sloop
- Year: 1720
- MSTR ID#: M-T-002
- SHIP ID#: S-E-006
- Captain/Master: David Tynes
- Passage 1: Start — Bermuda
- Arrival/Departure 2: Philadelphia [Pennsylvania] — 11 Aug 1720 / [25 Aug 1720] / [8 Sept 1720]
- > Bermuda
- Source: 5:88,92,96

Faro — Brigantine
- Year: 1723
- MSTR ID#: M-N-002
- SHIP ID#: S-F-001
- Captain/Master: Thomas New
- Passage 1: Start — Bristol [England]
- Arrival/Departure 2: Philadelphia [Pennsylvania] — [13 Jun 1723] / [4 Jul 1723]
- > Lisbon [Portugal]
- Source: 8:66,73
- Notes: (Known Passengers / Quaker) Philadelphia / Inward – 13 Jun 1723 – Count 1+

Fancy — Sloop
- Year: 1721
- MSTR ID#: M-H-005
- SHIP ID#: S-F-002
- Captain/Master: Crispin Hill
- Passage 1: Start — St Christopher's
- Arrival/Departure 2: Philadelphia [Pennsylvania] — 12 Aug 1721 / [21 Sept 1721]
- > Montserrat
- Source: 6:92,106

Fancy — Sloop
- Year: 1721
- MSTR ID#: M-W-003
- SHIP ID#: S-F-003
- Captain/Master: Thomas Wester
- Passage 1: Start — Barbados
- Arrival/Departure 2: St Martins
- > Philadelphia [Pennsylvania] — [9 Nov 1721]
- Source: 6:130

Group	Ship				Captain / Master		Passage	Arrival / Departure 1		Passage	Arrival / Departure 2		Page
	Year	Name	Type	Burden	First Name	Last Name	Length	Port	Arrival / Entered Inwards / Custom In / Entered Out	Length	Port	Arrival / Entered Inwards / Custom In / Entered Out	
F	MSTR ID#								Custom Out / Cleared Out			Custom Out / Cleared Out	12
	SHIP ID#	Registry Location						State / Country	Departure		State / Country	Departure	
	Source							Notes					

1720	Fazackerly	Sloop		George	Wilkinson	Start	Philadelphia	[1 Dec 1720] / [13 Dec 1720]	>		
M-W-004							[Pennsylvania]			Maryland	
S-F-004											
5:136,141											

1720	Fisher	Sloop		Richard	Sims	Start	Turks Island		>	Philadelphia	[28 Apr 1720] / [5 May 1720] / [26 May 1720]
M-S-006										[Pennsylvania]	
S-F-005						>	Barbados		>	Philadelphia	26 Aug 1720 / [8 Sept 1720] / [29 Sept 1720]
										[Pennsylvania]	
						>	Barbados				
5:41,45,53,56,94,96,107											

1720	Fortune	Ship		Richard	Stevens	Start	Exeter / Topsham		9 Weeks	Philadelphia	19 May 1720 / [9 Jun 1720] / [21 Jul 1720]
M-S-007							[England]			[Pennsylvania]	
S-F-006						>	Boston		>	Salem	[27 Aug 1720]
							[Massachusetts]			[New Jersey]	
						>	Spain				
5:53,56,60,79,96							(Known Passengers / Settlers) Philadelphia / Inward – 19 May 1720 – Count Many+				

1722 – 1723	Four Brothers	Sloop		Henry	Beeke	Start	Philadelphia	[5 Apr 1722] / [12 Apr 1722]	>	St Christopher's	
M-B-009							[Pennsylvania]				
S-F-007						>	Philadelphia	[19 Jul 1722] / [2 Aug 1722] / [9 Aug 1722]	>	St Christopher's	
							[Pennsylvania]				
						>	Philadelphia	[26 Dec 1722] / [14 Jan 1723] / [29 Jan 1723]	>	St Christopher's	
							[Pennsylvania]				
						>	Philadelphia	[16 May 1723] / [6 Jun 1723]	>	Antigua	
							[Pennsylvania]				
7:40,42,85,92,94,148 / 8:6,10,54,62											

Group	Ship				Captain / Master		Passage	Arrival / Departure 1			Passage	Arrival / Departure 2		Page
	Year	Name	Type	Burden	First Name	Last Name	Length	Port	Arrival / Entered Inwards / Custom In / Entered Out		Length	Port	Arrival / Entered Inwards / Custom In / Entered Out	13
F - G	MSTR ID#	Registry Location						State / Country	Custom Out / Cleared Out / Departure			State / Country	Custom Out / Cleared Out / Departure	
	SHIP ID#													
	Source								Notes					
	1720	Francis & Elizabeth	Sloop		John	Stammers	Start	Turks Island			>	Philadelphia	20 Apr 1720	
	M-S-008											[Pennsylvania]	[12 May 1720]	
	S-F-008						>	Jamaica						
	5:38,50													
	1722	Free Gift	Sloop		William	Dobbs	Start	New York	[11 Jun 1722]		>	Philadelphia	[28 Jun 1722]	
	M-D-001							[New York]	[11 Jun 1722]			[Pennsylvania]	[5 Jul 1722]	
	S-F-009						>	Boston	[23 Jul 1722] / [23 Jul 1722]		>	New York	[13 Aug 1722] / [15 Oct 1722]	
								[Massachusetts]				[New York]	XX [21 Oct 1722] XX / XXXXXXXXXXXXXX	
							>		Never Left For Port					
								Virginia	See Next Ship Or Captain					
	7:70,76,79,96 / 20:51													
	1723	Friendship	Sloop		George	Lambert	Start	St Christopher's			>	Philadelphia	[13 Jun 1723] / [4 Jul 1723]	
	M-L-001											[Pennsylvania]	[25 Jul 1723]	
	S-F-010						>	St Christopher's						
	8:66,73,81													
	1723	Gambole	Ship		Joseph	Ruddock	Start	Nevis			>	Philadelphia	[12 Sept 1723]	
	M-R-003											[Pennsylvania]	[31 Oct 1723]	
	S-G-001						>	Barbados						
	8:98,118													
	1723 – 1724	George	Ship		Henry	Wells	Start	Philadelphia	[25 Jul 1723]		>	Barbados		
	M-W-005							[Pennsylvania]	[29 Aug 1723]					
	S-G-002						>	Behire			>	Philadelphia	[7 Jan 1724]	
												[Pennsylvania]		
	8:81,94,142													

Group	Ship				Captain / Master		Passage	Arrival / Departure 1		Passage	Arrival / Departure 2		Page
G – H	Year	Name	Type	Burden	First Name	Last Name	Length	Port	Arrival / Entered Inwards	Length	Port	Arrival / Entered Inwards	14
	MSTR ID#								Custom In / Entered Out			Custom In / Entered Out	
	SHIP ID#	Registry Location						State / Country	Custom Out / Cleared Out		State / Country	Custom Out / Cleared Out	
		Source							Departure			Departure	
									Notes				

Year	Name	Type	Burden	First Name	Last Name	Length	Port	Arr/Dep 1	Length	Port	Arr/Dep 2
1722 – 1723	*Globe*	Ship	150 Tons	John	Mackay	Start	Holland		>	Dover [England]	
M-M-007											
S-G-003						>	Philadelphia [Pennsylvania]	[25 Oct 1722] [15 Nov 1722] [23 Nov 1722]	>	South Carolina	
						[>]	Holland		>	Dover [England]	
						>	Philadelphia [Pennsylvania]	[6 Sept 1723] [26 Sept 1723] [14 Nov 1723]	>	Lisbon [Portugal]	

7:122,132,136 / 8:96,100,103,104,110,126

(Known Passengers / Palatine) Philadelphia / Inward – 25 Oct 1722 – Count 120+
(Selling Palatine Boys) Philadelphia / Docked – Oct 1723 – Count 1+

Year	Name	Type	Burden	First Name	Last Name	Length	Port	Arr/Dep 1	Length	Port	Arr/Dep 2
1720	*Greyhound*	Sloop		Edward	Bailey	Start	St Christopher's		>	Philadelphia [Pennsylvania]	26 Jul 1720 [11 Aug 1720] [25 Aug 1720]
M-B-010											
S-G-004						>	St Christopher's				

5:82,88,92

Year	Name	Type	Burden	First Name	Last Name	Length	Port	Arr/Dep 1	Length	Port	Arr/Dep 2
1722	*Hamstead*	Sloop		Thomas	Randal	Start	New York [New York]	(13 Feb 1721) (27 Feb 1721)	>	Jamaica	
M-R-004											
S-H-001						>	New York [New York]	19 Jul 1721 [7 Aug 1721] [28 Aug 1721]	>	Jamaica	
						35 Days	New York [New York]	17 Nov 1721 (29 Jan 1722)	>	Jamaica	
						>	Philadelphia [Pennsylvania]	[24 May 1722] [7 Jun 1722]	>	New York [New York]	[18 Jun 1722] [16 Jul 1722] [30 Jul 1722]
						>	Jamaica				

6:20,23,84,90,96,137 / 7:13,60,68,74,85,92

Year	Name	Type	Burden	First Name	Last Name	Length	Port	Arr/Dep 1	Length	Port	Arr/Dep 2
1720	*Hopewell*	Sloop		John	Bartlett	Start	Boston [Massachusetts]		>	Philadelphia [Pennsylvania]	[23 Jun 1720] [30 Jun 1720] [14 Jul 1720]
M-B-038											
S-H-018						>	Boston [Massachusetts]	[10 Sept 1720]	>	Philadelphia [Pennsylvania]	

5:67,70,75,106

Group	Year	Ship Name	Type	Burden	Captain/Master First Name	Captain/Master Last Name	Passage Length	Port / State Country	Arrival/Departure 1	Passage Length	Port / State Country	Arrival/Departure 2	Page
	MSTR ID# / SHIP ID#	Registry Location / Source							Arrival / Entered Inwards / Custom In / Entered Out / Custom Out / Cleared Out / Departure			Notes	

Group H													Page 15

Hamstead Galley — 1720–1722, Ship — M-W-006 / S-H-002

	Port	Arrival/Departure 1	Passage	Port	Arrival/Departure 2
Captain: Francis Wells	Philadelphia [Pennsylvania]	[31 Mar 1720] / [5 May 1720]	>	Jamaica	
[>]	London [England]	[? Jun 1721]	11 Weeks	Philadelphia [Pennsylvania]	[7 Sept 1721] / [30 Nov 1721] / [19 Apr 1722]
>	Jamaica				

Source: 5:32,45 / 6:90,100,138 / 7:46 / Cargo 6:125,130,140

Hannah — 1723, Sloop — M-L-002 / S-H-003

	Port	Arrival/Departure 1	Passage	Port	Arrival/Departure 2
Captain: Thomas Lowtor — Start	Boston [Massachusetts]		>	Philadelphia [Pennsylvania]	[17 Dec 1723] / [24 Dec 1723]
>	Boston [Massachusetts]				

Source: 8:136,138

Hawk — 1723, Sloop — M-B-011 / S-H-004

	Port	Arrival/Departure 1	Passage	Port	Arrival/Departure 2
Captain: Robert Bloom — Start	Barbados		>	Philadelphia [Pennsylvania]	[25 Jul 1723] / [22 Aug 1723] / [4 Oct 1723]
>	Barbados				

Source: 8:81,91,106

Henry — 1721, Sloop — M-B-012 / S-H-005

	Port	Arrival/Departure 1	Passage	Port	Arrival/Departure 2
Captain: Bristow Brown — Start	Bermuda		>	Philadelphia [Pennsylvania]	[2 Nov 1721] / [9 Nov 1721] / [30 Nov 1721]
>	Jamaica				

Source: 6:125,130,138

Henry — 1721, Sloop — M-M-008 / S-H-006

	Port	Arrival/Departure 1	Passage	Port	Arrival/Departure 2
Captain: John Manners — Start	Patuxent Maryland		>	Philadelphia [Pennsylvania]	14 Jul 1721 / [20 Jul 1721] / [27 Jul 1721]
>	Patuxent Maryland		>	Philadelphia [Pennsylvania]	28 Aug 1721 / [31 Aug 1721] / [7 Sept 1721]
>	Patuxent Maryland				

Source: 6:79,84,96

Group	Year / MSTR ID# / SHIP ID#	Name / Registry Location	Type	Burden	First Name	Last Name	Length	Port / State/Country	Arrival / Entered Inwards — Custom In / Entered Out — Custom Out / Cleared Out — Departure	Length	Port / State/Country	Arrival / Entered Inwards — Custom In / Entered Out — Custom Out / Cleared Out — Departure	Page
H – I	1722 – 1723 / M-W-007 / S-H-007	Hope	Sloop		Jehoshaphat / Joseph	Wellman / Willman	Start	Bermuda		>	Philadelphia / [Pennsylvania]	[10 May 1722] / [17 May 1722] / [24 May 1722]	16
							>	Madeira Island / [Portugal]					
							NO SUPPORTING DATA TO LINK TIMELINE						
							Start	Bermuda		>	Philadelphia / [Pennsylvania]	[25 Apr 1723] / [25 Apr 1723] / [9 May 1723]	
							>	Madeira Island / [Portugal]					
	Source: 7:54,58,60 / 8:42,50												

Group	Year / MSTR ID# / SHIP ID#	Name	Type	Burden	First Name	Last Name	Length	Port / State/Country	Notes	Length	Port / State/Country		Page
	1722 / M-H-006 / S-H-008	Hoy Delaware			Samuel	Hayman	Start	Philadelphia / [Pennsylvania]	[19 Jul 1722] / [19 Jul 1722]	>	North Carolina		
	Source: 7:85												

	1720 – 1722 / M-V-001 / S-I-001	Illustrious	Ship		Henry	Virr	Start	Bristol / [England]		>	Philadelphia / [Pennsylvania]	13 Nov 1720 / [1 Dec 1720] / [20 Dec 1720]	
							>	Jamaica		[>]	Bristol / [England]	29 Aug or 4 Sept 1721	
							>	Delaware River	[2 Nov 1721]	>	Philadelphia / [Pennsylvania]	[9 Nov 1721] / [23 Nov 1721] / XX [29 Mar 1722] XX / XXXXXXXXXXXXXX	
							>	Jamaica	Never Left For Port / See Next Ship Or Captain				
							XXXXXXXXXX Changed Departure Location XXXXXXXXXX						
							Start	Philadelphia / [Pennsylvania]	XXXXXXXXXXXXXX / XX [23 Nov 1721] XX / [29 Mar 1722]	>	Barbados		
	Source: 5:129,136 / 6:2,125,130,134 / 7:38												

	1720 / M-P-003 / S-I-002	Industry	Sloop		Joseph	Palmer	Start	South Carolina		>	Philadelphia / [Pennsylvania]	[19 May 1720] / [19 May 1720] / [1 Jun 1720]	
							>	South Carolina	Never Reached Port / Taken / Spanish Privateer	>	St Augustine / [Florida]	[? Jun 1720] / Carried Into This Port	
							>	Charles Town / South Carolina	31 Jul 1720 / Released As Prisoner				
	Source: 5:53,58,88,138												

Group	Ship				Captain / Master		Passage	Arrival / Departure 1		Passage	Arrival / Departure 2		Page
	Year	Name	Type	Burden	First Name	Last Name	Length	Port	Arrival / Entered Inwards	Length	Port	Arrival / Entered Inwards	
									Custom In / Entered Out			Custom In / Entered Out	
J	MSTR ID#							State / Country	Custom Out / Cleared Out		State / Country	Custom Out / Cleared Out	17
	SHIP ID#	Registry Location							Departure			Departure	
	Source							Notes					

	1721	James & Mary	Ship		John	Ball	Start	St Christopher's		>	Philadelphia	10 Aug 1721	
	M-B-013										[Pennsylvania]	[7 Sept 1721]	
	S-J-001											[7 Sept 1721]	
							>	Virginia					
	6:92,100												

	1721	Jane	Brigantine		William	Rime / Rimes	Start	Barbados		>	Philadelphia	2 May 1721	
	M-R-005										[Pennsylvania]	[29 Jun 1721]	
	S-J-002												
							>	Madeira Island					
								[Portugal]					
	6:44,56,67												

	1720	Jane	Sloop		John	Phipps	Start	North Carolina		>	Philadelphia	8 Oct 1720	
	M-P-004										[Pennsylvania]	[27 Oct 1720]	
	S-J-003												
							>	North Carolina					
	5:112,120												

	1720	Jenny	Ship		Thomas	Tudor	Start	Barbados		>	Philadelphia	5 Oct 1720	
	M-T-006										[Pennsylvania]	[20 Oct 1720]	
	S-J-004												
							>	Barbados					
	5:110,115												

	1723	Jeremiah	Scallop		John	Wood	Start			>	Philadelphia	[26 Sept 1723]	
	M-W-008							Maryland			[Pennsylvania]		
	S-J-005												
	8:103												

	1720	John	Sloop		Henry	Friend	Start	St Christopher's		>	Philadelphia	26 Jul 1720	
	M-F-003										[Pennsylvania]	[25 Aug 1720]	
	S-J-006												
							>	Jamaica					
	5:82,92												

Group		Ship				Captain / Master		Passage	Arrival / Departure 1		Passage	Arrival / Departure 2		Page
	Year	Name	Type	Burden	First Name	Last Name	Length	Port	Arrival / Entered Inwards	Length	Port	Arrival / Entered Inwards		
	MSTR ID#								Custom In / Entered Out			Custom In / Entered Out		
J	SHIP ID#	Registry Location						State / Country	Custom Out / Cleared Out		State / Country	Custom Out / Cleared Out		18
									Departure			Departure		
	Source							Notes						

1720 – 1723		*John & Mary*	Sloop				Start	Delaware River		>	New York	27 Jun 1720	
M-C-003					John	Clarke						[10 Oct 1720]	
S-J-007											[New York]	[17 Oct 1720]	
							>	Boston		>			
								[Massachusetts]			Rhode Island		
							>	New York	24 Nov 1720	[>]	New Castle		
								[New York]			[Delaware]		
							>	New York	[3 Jul 1721]	[>]	Lewes		
								[New York]			[Delaware]		
							>	New York	[14 Aug 1721]	[>]	New Castle		
								[New York]			[Delaware]		
							>	New York	(19 Dec 1721)	[>]	New Castle		
								[New York]			[Delaware]		
							>	New York	[21 Apr 1722]	[>]	Lewes		
								[New York]			[Delaware]		
							>	New York	13 Jul 1722	[>]	New Castle		
								[New York]			[Delaware]		
							>	New York	10 Sept 1722	[>]	New Castle		
								[New York]			[Delaware]		
							>	New York	(24 Dec 1722)	>	Philadelphia	[5 Feb 1723]	
								[New York]			[Pennsylvania]		
							>	Port Lewis		>	Curacao		
								[Delaware]					
							>	New York	4 Jun 1723	>	Placentia		
									[17 Jun 1723]				
								[New York]	[24 Jun 1723]		Newfoundland		
							1 Month	New York	19 Sept 1723	>	Philadelphia	[11 Oct 1723]	
								[New York]			[Pennsylvania]	[24 Oct 1723]	
							>	New Castle		>	New York	18 Nov 1723	
								[Delaware]			[New York]		

5:70,112,115,136 / 6:71,92,148 / 7:48,85,108,151 / 8:12,16,65,68,70,106,109,114,130

Group	Ship				Captain / Master		Passage	Arrival / Departure 1		Passage	Arrival / Departure 2		Page
	Year	Name	Type	Burden	First Name	Last Name	Length	Port	Arrival / Entered Inwards	Length	Port	Arrival / Entered Inwards	
J – L									Custom In / Entered Out			Custom In / Entered Out	19
	MSTR ID#								Custom Out / Cleared Out			Custom Out / Cleared Out	
	SHIP ID#	Registry Location						State / Country	Departure		State / Country	Departure	
	Source							Notes					

	1720	John & Thomas	Sloop		Henry	White	Start	Providence		>	Philadelphia	[9 Jun 1720] [7 Jul 1720]	
	M-W-009										[Pennsylvania]	[21 Jul 1720]	
	S-J-008												
							>	Providence					
	5:60,72,79												

	1722	Joseph & John	Brigantine		Peter	Peters	Start	Philadelphia		>			
	M-P-005							[Pennsylvania]	[5 Jul 1722]		Maryland		
	S-J-009												
	7:79												

	1723	Kings Fisher	Schooner		Richard	Barrington	Start	Boston	[12 Oct 1723] [19 Oct 1723]	>	Philadelphia	[21 Nov 1723] [29 Nov 1723]	
	M-B-014							[Massachusetts]			[Pennsylvania]		
	S-K-001												
							>	New Castle					
								Delaware					
	8:128,130 / 20:115,116												

	1719 – 1722	Little Anne	Sloop		Samuel	Bignell / Bignall / Bicknall	Start	Philadelphia		>	Jamaica		
	M-B-015							[Pennsylvania]	[29 Dec 1719]				
	S-L-001												
							35 Days	Philadelphia	1 Aug 1720 [6 Oct 1720]	>	Suriname		
								[Pennsylvania]				2 Feb 1721	
							>	Philadelphia	17 Mar 1721 [30 Mar 1721] [30 Mar 1721]	>	Boston		
								[Pennsylvania]			[Massachusetts]		
							>	Philadelphia	[15 Jun 1721] [15 Jun 1721] [6 Jul 1721]	>	Jamaica		
								[Pennsylvania]					
							>	Philadelphia	[19 Oct 1721] [30 Nov 1721] [7 Dec 1721]	>	Madeira Island		
								[Pennsylvania]			[Portugal]		
							>	Philadelphia	[29 Mar 1722] [5 Apr 1722] [3 May 1722]	>	Jamaica		
								[Pennsylvania]					
							>	Philadelphia	[16 Aug 1722] [10 Oct 1722] [23 Nov 1722]	>	Jamaica		
								[Pennsylvania]					
	5:4,86,110 / 6:32,34,60,71,120,138,140 / 7:38,40,52,96,118,136							(Known Passengers) Philadelphia / Inward – 19 Oct 1721 – Count 1+					

Group	Ship				Captain / Master		Passage	Arrival / Departure 1		Passage	Arrival / Departure 2		Page
	Year	Name	Type	Burden	First Name	Last Name	Length	Port	Arrival / Entered Inwards / Custom In / Entered Out	Length	Port	Arrival / Entered Inwards / Custom In / Entered Out	
L	MSTR ID#								Custom Out / Cleared Out			Custom Out / Cleared Out	20
	SHIP ID#	Registry Location						State / Country	Departure		State / Country	Departure	
	Source							Notes					

1720	Lennox Galley	Ship		James	Vance	Start	Philadelphia	[14 Mar 1720] / [14 Mar 1720]	>	Bristol	
M-V-002											
S-L-002							[Pennsylvania]			[England]	
5:27											

1720 – 1723	London Hope	Ship		John	Annis	Start	London		>	Downs	Departed Before [8 Mar 1720]
M-A-004											
S-L-003							[England]			[England]	
						>	Philadelphia	[12 May 1720] / [26 May 1720] / [4 Aug 1720]	>	London	
							[Pennsylvania]			[England]	
						>	Philadelphia	20 Jun 1721 / [27 Jul 1721] / [16 Nov 1721]	>	English Channel	28 Dec 1721
							[Pennsylvania]				
						>	London		>	Delaware River	7 Jun 1722
							[England]				
						>	Philadelphia	[14 Jun 1722] / [21 Jun 1722] / [8 Nov 1722]	>	London	
							[Pennsylvania]			[England]	
						>	Philadelphia	[27 Jun 1723] / [11 Jul 1723] / [11 Oct 1723]	>	London	
							[Pennsylvania]			[England]	
5:50,56,86 / 6:63,84,132 / 7:38,68,70,74,130 / 8:70,76,109							(Selling Servants) Philadelphia / Docked - 22 Aug 1723 - Count 1+				

1720	Love	Sloop		Francis	Saltus	Start	Turks Island		>	Philadelphia	8 Aug 1720 / [25 Aug 1720] / [25 Aug 1720]
M-S-009											
S-L-004										[Pennsylvania]	
						>	Bermuda		>		
						NO SUPPORTING DATA TO LINK TIMELINE					

1722	Love	Sloop				Start	Bermuda		>	Philadelphia	[12 Apr 1722] / [3 May 1722] / [17 May 1722]
S-L-004										[Pennsylvania]	
						>	Barbados		>		
5:88,92 / 7:42,52,58											

Group	Ship				Captain / Master		Passage	Arrival / Departure 1		Passage	Arrival / Departure 2		Page
	Year	Name	Type	Burden	First Name	Last Name	Length	Port	Arrival / Entered Inwards / Custom In / Entered Out	Length	Port	Arrival / Entered Inwards / Custom In / Entered Out	
L – M	MSTR ID#	Registry Location						State / Country	Custom Out / Cleared Out / Departure		State / Country	Custom Out / Cleared Out / Departure	21
	SHIP ID#	Source							Notes				

Group	Year	Name	Type	Burden	MSTR ID# / SHIP ID#	First Name	Last Name	Passage Length	Port	State/Country	Dates	Passage Length	Port	State/Country	Dates
	1720 – 1721	*Lydia*	Sloop		M-P-006 / S-L-005	Peter	Peters	Start	Antigua			>	Philadelphia	[Pennsylvania]	30 Jun 1720 / [14 Jul 1720] / [21 Jul 1720]
								>	North Carolina			[>]	Anguilla		
								>	Philadelphia	[Pennsylvania]	11 Apr 1721 / [20 Apr 1721] / [27 Apr 1721]	>	St Christopher's		
	Source: 5:72,75,78,79 / 6:38,40,42														
	1720	*MacCollum*	Ship		M-L-003 / S-M-001	Charles	Lynn	Start	Philadelphia	[Pennsylvania]	[2 Feb 1720]	>	Bristol	[England]	
	Source: 5:14														
	1723	*Martha & Elizabeth*	Ship		M-W-010 / S-M-003	James	Willocks	Start	Londonderry	[Ireland]		>	Philadelphia	[Pennsylvania]	[14 Nov 1723] / [24 Dec 1723]
								>	Barbados						
	Source: 8:126,138														
	1721	*Mary*	Brigantine		M-S-011 / S-M-004	Stephen	Seavy	Start	St Christopher's			>	Philadelphia	[Pennsylvania]	29 May 1721 / [13 Jul 1721]
								>	Madeira Island	[Portugal]					
	Source: 6:56,76														
	1722	*Mary*	Sloop		M-S-012 / S-M-005	John	Stout	Start	Barbados			>	Philadelphia	[Pennsylvania]	[26 Apr 1722] / [17 May 1722] / [31 May 1722]
								>	Barbados						
	Source: 7:48,58,64														

Group	Year	Ship Name	Type	Burden	Captain First Name	Captain Last Name	Passage Length	Port	State / Country	Arrival / Entered Inwards	Custom In / Entered Out	Custom Out / Cleared Out	Departure	Passage Length	Port	State / Country	Arrival / Entered Inwards	Custom In / Entered Out	Custom Out / Cleared Out	Departure	Page
M	1722 – 1723 / M-B-016 / S-M-006 / 7:132,138 / 8:28,34 / 20:91,92,93	Mary	Sloop		James	Brown	Start	Philadelphia	[Pennsylvania]	[15 Nov 1722]	[29 Nov 1722]			>	Antigua						22
							>	Philadelphia	[Pennsylvania]	[21 Mar 1723]	[4 Apr 1723]			>	Boston	[Massachusetts]	[27 Apr 1723]	[4 May 1723]	[11 May 1723]		
							>	Philadelphia	[Pennsylvania]												
M	1723 / M-R-006 / S-M-007 / 8:138	Mary	Sloop		John	Read	Start	Philadelphia	[Pennsylvania]		[24 Dec 1723]			>	Jamaica						
M	1723 / M-D-002 / S-M-008 / 8:24,50,54,60	Mary	Sloop		Jonathan	Dickinson	Start	Barbados						18 Days	Rhode Island		8 Feb 1723				
							[>]	Barbados						16 Days	Philadelphia	[Pennsylvania]	9 May 1723	[16 May 1723]	[30 May 1723]		
							>	Rhode Island													
M	1720 / M-G-006 / S-M-009 / 5:50,56,67	Mary	Sloop		Francis	Giffing	Start	Barbados						>	Philadelphia	[Pennsylvania]	[12 May 1720]	[26 May 1720]	[23 Jun 1720]		
							>	Barbados													
M	1720 / M-B-017 / S-M-010 / 5:53	Mary	Ship		William	Beran	Start		Ireland					>	Philadelphia	[Pennsylvania]	[19 May 1720]				
M	1723 / M-J-002 / S-M-011 / 8:88,96	Mary	Sloop		Thomas	James	Start	Philadelphia	[Pennsylvania]	[15 Aug 1723]	[6 Sept 1723]			>	Jamaica						

Group	Ship				Captain / Master		Passage	Arrival / Departure 1		Passage	Arrival / Departure 2		Page
	Year	Name	Type	Burden	First Name	Last Name	Length	Port	Arrival/Entered Inwards; Custom In/Entered Out; Custom Out/Cleared Out; Departure	Length	Port	Arrival/Entered Inwards; Custom In/Entered Out; Custom Out/Cleared Out; Departure	
	MSTR ID# / SHIP ID#	Registry Location						State / Country			State / Country	Notes	
M													23
	1722	Mary	Ship		James	Straiton / Straton	Start			>	Philadelphia	[14 Jun 1722] [14 Jun 1722] [19 Jul 1722]	
	M-S-013 / S-M-012							Scotland			[Pennsylvania]		
								London		>			
								[England]					
	Source: 7:70,85												
	1722	Mary & Anne	Sloop		William	Burn	Start			>	Philadelphia	[29 Mar 1722] [12 Apr 1722] [3 May 1722]	
	M-B-018 / S-M-013							Rhode Island			[Pennsylvania]		
								Rhode Island		>			
	Source: 7:38,42,52												
	1721	Mary & Catherine	Brigantine		Sylvan	Fry	Start	Montserrat		>	Philadelphia	5 Aug 1721	
	M-F-004 / S-M-014										[Pennsylvania]	[2 Nov 1721]	
								Montserrat		>			
	Source: 6:90,125												
	1720	Mary Galley	Ship		Robert	Liston	Start	Philadelphia	[2 Feb 1720] [7 Mar 1720]	>	Barbados		
	M-L-004 / S-M-015							[Pennsylvania]					
	Source: 5:14,24												
	1721 – 1722	Mayflower	Schooner		Charles	Blakey	Start	Philadelphia	[30 Mar 1721] [6 Apr 1721]	>	Jamaica		
	M-B-019 / S-M-016							[Pennsylvania]					
							>	Philadelphia	18 Jul 1721 [27 Jul 1721] [3 Aug 1721]	>	Jamaica		
								[Pennsylvania]					
							[>]	South Carolina		>	Philadelphia	[19 Apr 1722] [10 May 1722] [14 Jun 1722]	
											[Pennsylvania]		
							>	Jamaica					
	Source: 6:32,34,36,79,84,87 / 7:46,54,70												

Group	Ship				Captain / Master		Passage	Arrival / Departure 1		Passage	Arrival / Departure 2		Page
	Year	Name	Type	Burden	First Name	Last Name	Length	Port	Arrival / Entered Inwards	Length	Port	Arrival / Entered Inwards	
M									Custom In / Entered Out			Custom In / Entered Out	24
	MSTR ID#							State / Country	Custom Out / Cleared Out		State / Country	Custom Out / Cleared Out	
	SHIP ID#	Registry Location							Departure			Departure	
	Source							Notes					

1720 – 1721	*Mayflower*	Sloop			Thomas	Ainsworth	Start	Antigua		>	Philadelphia	[26 May 1720] [9 Jun 1720]	
M-A-005											[Pennsylvania]	[30 Jun 1720]	
S-M-017													
							>	Jamaica		>	Philadelphia	26 Nov 1720 [1 Dec 1720]	
											[Pennsylvania]	[20 Dec 1720]	
							>	Barbados		[>]	Antigua		
							>	Philadelphia	17 Jun 1721 [21 Jun 1721]	>	Barbados		
								[Pennsylvania]	[20 Jul 1721]				
5:56,60,70,136 / 6:2,63,79													

1720	*Mayflower*	Schooner			Phillip	Barger	Start	North Carolina		>	Lewis Town		
M-B-020											[Delaware]		
S-M-018													
							>	Philadelphia	21 Jul 1720				
								[Pennsylvania]					
5:82													

1721 – 1722	*Milford Galley*	Ship			Edward	Foy	Start	Bristol		>	Milford Haven		
M-F-005								[England]			[Wales]		
S-M-019	Bristol, England												
							>	Philadelphia	[23 Nov 1721]	>	Port Royal	28 Aug 1722	
								[Pennsylvania]	[5 Apr 1722]		Jamaica	Overturned	
							&	Men Saved		>	Port Royal	Lost In Harbor / Hurricane	
								Ship Was Lost			Jamaica		
6:134 / 7:40,146													

1720	*Modena*	Sloop			Samuel	Harvey	Start	St Martins		>	Providence		
M-H-007													
S-M-020													
							>	Philadelphia	26 Aug 1720 [22 Sept 1720]	>	Jamaica		
								[Pennsylvania]	[29 Sept 1720]				
5:94,103,107													

Group	Ship				Captain / Master		Passage	Arrival / Departure 1		Passage	Arrival / Departure 2		Page
M – N	Year	Name	Type	Burden	First Name	Last Name	Length	Port / Arrival–Entered Inwards / Custom In–Entered Out / Custom Out–Cleared Out / Departure / State–Country		Length	Port / State–Country / dates		25
	MSTR ID# / SHIP ID#	Registry Location											
	Source							Notes					

Montrose — M-L-005 / S-M-021

Year	Name	Type	First Name	Last Name	Length	Port / State-Country	Dates	Length	Port / State-Country	Dates
1719 – 1721	Montrose	Brigantine	David	Lindsey	Start	Philadelphia [Pennsylvania]	[22 Dec 1719]	>	Jamaica	
					>	Philadelphia [Pennsylvania]	[7 Apr 1720] [28 Apr 1720] [26 May 1720]	>	Madeira Island [Portugal]	
					>	Philadelphia [Pennsylvania]	18 Sept 1720 [3 Nov 1720] [1 Dec 1720]	>	Madeira Island [Portugal]	
					[>]	Barbados		>	Philadelphia [Pennsylvania]	[18 May 1721] [29 Jun 1721] [27 Jul 1721]
					>	Montrose [Scotland]				

Source: 5:2,34,41,56,103,123,136 / 6:49,67,84

Nancy — M-B-021 / S-N-001

Year	Name	Type	First Name	Last Name	Length	Port / State-Country	Dates	Length	Port / State-Country	Dates
1720 – 1722	Nancy	Snow	John	Bedford	Start	Bristol [England]	10 Jul 1720	>	Philadelphia [Pennsylvania]	6 Sept 1720 [29 Sept 1720]
					>	Bristol [England]	31 Mar 1721	>	Philadelphia [Pennsylvania]	14 Jun 1721 [13 Jul 1721] [31 Aug 1721]
					>	Bristol [England]		>	Philadelphia [Pennsylvania]	[26 Apr 1722] [10 May 1722] [14 Jun 1722]
					>	Antigua				

Source: 5:96,107,110 / 6:60,76,96 / 7:48,54,70

Notes: (Known Passengers / Servants) Philadelphia / Inward – 14 Jun 1721 – Count [Great Many]

Neptune — M-V-003 / S-N-002

Year	Name	Type	First Name	Last Name	Length	Port / State-Country	Dates	Length	Port / State-Country	Dates
1720 – 1723	Neptune	Ship	Abraham	Vinning	Start	Philadelphia [Pennsylvania]	[7 Mar 1720] [5 May 1720]	>	Barbados	
					>	Philadelphia [Pennsylvania]	5 Sept 1720 [29 Sept 1720] [8 Dec 1720]	>	London [England]	
					>	Downs [England]	15 Jul 1721	>	Philadelphia [Pennsylvania]	[26 Oct 1721] [26 Jul 1722] [27 Sept 1722]
					>	Bristol [England]		[>]	Jamaica	
					>	Philadelphia [Pennsylvania]	[8 Aug 1723]			

Source: 5:24,45,96,107,110,138 / 6:108,122 / 7:89,112 / 8:86

Group	Ship				Captain / Master		Passage	Arrival / Departure 1		Passage	Arrival / Departure 2		Page
	Year	Name	Type	Burden	First Name	Last Name	Length	Port	Arrival / Entered Inwards	Length	Port	Arrival / Entered Inwards	
N	MSTR ID#								Custom In / Entered Out			Custom In / Entered Out	26
	SHIP ID#	Registry Location						State / Country	Custom Out / Cleared Out		State / Country	Custom Out / Cleared Out	
									Departure			Departure	
	Source							Notes					

Year	Name	Type	Burden	First Name	Last Name	Length	Port	Arr/Dep 1 dates	Length	Port	Arr/Dep 2 dates
1720	Neptune	Sloop		Thomas	Cheesman	Start	Barbados		>	Philadelphia	18 Jun 1720 / [30 Jun 1720] / [28 Jul 1720]
M-C-004										[Pennsylvania]	
S-N-003						>	Barbados				
5:67,70,82											

Year	Name	Type	Burden	First Name	Last Name	Length	Port	Arr/Dep 1 dates	Length	Port	Arr/Dep 2 dates
1722	Neptune	Sloop		William	Swain	Start			>	Philadelphia	[16 Aug 1722] / [13 Sept 1722] / [27 Sept 1722]
M-S-014							Rhode Island			[Pennsylvania]	
S-N-004						>	Rhode Island				
7:96,108,112											

Year	Name	Type	Burden	First Name	Last Name	Length	Port	Arr/Dep 1 dates	Length	Port	Arr/Dep 2 dates
1720	Newport	Sloop		John	Brewer	Start			>		[18 Mar 1720]
M-B-022							Virginia			[Rhode Island]	[8 Apr 1720]
S-N-005						>	Philadelphia	[28 Apr 1720]	>		
							[Pennsylvania]	[19 May 1720]		[Rhode Island]	
5:34,38,41,53											

Year	Name	Type	Burden	First Name	Last Name	Length	Port	Arr/Dep 1 dates	Length	Port	Arr/Dep 2 dates
1723	Newport	Sloop		Johannes	De Haes	Start	St Christopher's		>	Philadelphia	[30 May 1723] / [13 Jun 1723]
M-D-003										[Pennsylvania]	
S-N-006						>	St Christopher's				
8:60,66											

Year	Name	Type	Burden	First Name	Last Name	Length	Port	Arr/Dep 1 dates	Length	Port	Arr/Dep 2 dates
1723	Newport	Sloop		William	Griffith	Start	Antigua		>	Philadelphia	[11 Oct 1723] / [21 Nov 1723] / [5 Dec 1723]
M-G-007										[Pennsylvania]	
S-N-007						>	Antigua				
8:109,128,132											

Group	Ship				Captain / Master		Passage	Arrival / Departure 1		Passage	Arrival / Departure 2		Page
	Year	Name	Type	Burden	First Name	Last Name	Length	Port	Arrival / Entered Inwards / Custom In / Entered Out	Length	Port	Arrival / Entered Inwards / Custom In / Entered Out	
N – P	MSTR ID#	Registry Location						State / Country	Custom Out / Cleared Out / Departure		State / Country	Custom Out / Cleared Out / Departure	27
	SHIP ID#												
	Source								Notes				

Nightingale — Sloop
MSTR ID# M-A-006, SHIP ID# S-N-008, Year 1720 – 1721
Captain: Anthony Attwood

Passage	Port	Dates	Passage	Port	Dates
Start	St Christopher's		>	Philadelphia [Pennsylvania]	[9 Jun 1720] [30 Jun 1720] [21 Jul 1720]
>	St Christopher's		[>]	Boston [Massachusetts]	
>	Philadelphia [Pennsylvania]	21 Nov 1720 [24 Nov 1720] [13 Dec 1720]	>	St Christopher's	
>	Philadelphia [Pennsylvania]	[13 Apr 1721] [27 Apr 1721] [18 May 1721]	>	St Christopher's	

Source: 5:60,70,79,133,138,141 / 6:38,42,49

Olive Branch — Sloop
MSTR ID# M-B-024, SHIP ID# S-O-001, Year 1723
Captain: Daniel Burch

Passage	Port	Dates	Passage	Port	Dates
Start	Turks Island		>	Philadelphia [Pennsylvania]	[4 Jul 1723] [11 Jul 1723] [25 Jul 1723]
>	Barbados				

Source: 8:73,76,81

Owners Goodwill — Ship
MSTR ID# M-H-008, SHIP ID# S-O-002, Year 1723 – 1724
Captain: William Hawarden

Passage	Port	Dates	Passage	Port	Dates
Start	St Christopher's		>	Philadelphia [Pennsylvania]	[9 Dec 1723] [7 Jan 1724]
>	St Christopher's				

Source: 8:134,142

Philadelphia — Ship
MSTR ID# M-H-009, SHIP ID# S-P-001, Year 1720
Captain: John Hopkins

Passage	Port	Dates	Passage	Port	Dates
Start	Bristol [England]		>	Philadelphia [Pennsylvania]	[9 Jun 1720] [14 Jul 1720] [28 Jul 1720]
>	York River [Virginia]				

Source: 5:60,75,82

Philadelphia — Ship
MSTR ID# M-B-023, SHIP ID# S-P-002, Year 1722 – 1723
Captain: Thomas Boutne / Bourne

Passage	Port	Dates	Passage	Port	Dates
Start	Bristol [England]		>	Philadelphia [Pennsylvania]	[10 May 1722] [28 Jun 1722] [16 Aug 1722]
>	Bristol [England]		>	Philadelphia [Pennsylvania]	[23 May 1723] [4 Jul 1723]
>	[Virginia]				

Source: 7:54,76,96 / 8:58,73

Group					Captain / Master		Passage	Arrival / Departure 1		Passage	Arrival / Departure 2		Page
P	Year	Name	Type	Burden	First Name	Last Name	Length	Port	Arrival / Entered Inwards · Custom In / Entered Out	Length	Port	Arrival / Entered Inwards · Custom In / Entered Out	**28**
	MSTR ID# / SHIP ID#	Registry Location						State / Country	Custom Out / Cleared Out · Departure		State / Country	Custom Out / Cleared Out · Departure	
	Source							Notes					

Record 1

Year	Name	Type	Burden	MSTR ID#	SHIP ID#	First Name	Last Name	Passage	Port 1	State/Country 1	Passage	Port 2	State/Country 2	Dates 2
1720	Philadelphia	Sloop		M-R-007	S-P-003	Nicholas	Roach	Start		North Carolina	>	Philadelphia	[Pennsylvania]	[5 May 1720] / [1 Jun 1720] / [1 Jun 1720]
								>		North Carolina	>	Philadelphia	[Pennsylvania]	8 Oct 1720

Source: 5:45,58,112

Record 2

Year	Name	Type	MSTR ID#	SHIP ID#	First Name	Last Name	Passage	Port 1	State/Country 1	Dates 1	Passage	Arrival/Departure 2
1720	Philadelphia	Sloop	M-C-005	S-P-004	Jonathan	Cropper	Start	Crooked Island	Bahamas	[? Mar 1720] / Drove on Shore	&	5 Men of Ships Crew Saved / Rest Of Ships Crew & Ship Was Lost
							>	Philadelphia	[Pennsylvania]	14 Sept 1720 / Carried Into This Port		

Source: 5:99

Notes: Saved By – Sloop William: Captain Hurst – Taken To Philadelphia, Pennsylvania

Record 3

Year	Name	Type	MSTR ID#	SHIP ID#	First Name	Last Name	Passage	Port 1	State/Country 1	Passage	Port 2	State/Country 2	Dates 2
1721	Philadelphia	Schooner	M-D-004	S-P-005	John	Drake	Start	Boston	[Massachusetts]	>	Philadelphia	[Pennsylvania]	[6 Jul 1721] / [13 Jul 1721] / [27 Jul 1721]
							>	Boston	[Massachusetts]				

Source: 6:71,76,84

Record 4

Year	Name	Type	MSTR ID#	SHIP ID#	First Name	Last Name	Passage	Port 1	State/Country 1	Dates 1	Passage	Port 2	State/Country 2
1722	Peggy	Sloop	M-H-011	S-P-006	Benjamin	Harris	Start	Philadelphia	[Pennsylvania]	[27 Feb 1722]	>		South Carolina

Source: 7:23

Record 5

Year	Name	Type	MSTR ID#	SHIP ID#	First Name	Last Name	Passage	Port 1	State/Country 1	Passage	Port 2	State/Country 2	Dates 2
1722 – 1723	Pembroke	Ship	M-H-010	S-P-007	John	Hopkins	Start	Bristol	[England]	>	Philadelphia	[Pennsylvania]	[1 Nov 1722] / [18 Dec 1722]
							>	Barbados		[>]	Philadelphia	[Pennsylvania]	[18 Apr 1723]
							>	Barbados					

Source: 7:126,146 / 8:40

Notes: (Known Passengers / Welsh & West Country Servants) Philadelphia / Inward – 1 Nov 1722 – Count 30+

Record 6

Year	Name	Type	MSTR ID#	SHIP ID#	First Name	Last Name	Passage	Port 1	State/Country 1	Passage	Port 2	State/Country 2	Dates 2
1723	Princess	Snow	M-G-008	S-P-008	Paul	Garmston	Start	Bristol	[England]	>	Philadelphia	[Pennsylvania]	[31 Oct 1723] / [5 Dec 1723]
							>	Madeira Island	[Portugal]				

Source: 8:118,132

Group	Ship				Captain / Master		Passage	Arrival / Departure 1		Passage	Arrival / Departure 2		Page
	Year	Name	Type	Burden	First Name	Last Name	Length	Port	Arrival / Entered Inwards / Custom In / Entered Out	Length	Port	Arrival / Entered Inwards / Custom In / Entered Out	29
P	MSTR ID#	Registry Location						State / Country	Custom Out / Cleared Out / Departure		State / Country	Custom Out / Cleared Out / Departure	
	SHIP ID#												
	Source							Notes					

	1720	*Prince of Orange*	Ship		Edward	Sparks	Start	Milford Haven		>	Philadelphia	[26 May 1720] [16 Jun 1720] [7 Jul 1720]	
	M-S-015							[Wales]			[Pennsylvania]		
	S-P-009												
							>	Barbados		[>]	Antigua		
							>	Philadelphia	9 Nov 1720 [8 Dec 1720] [20 Dec 1720]	>	St Augustine		
								[Pennsylvania]			[Florida]		
	5:56,63,72,126,136 / 6:2							(Known Passengers / Prisoners) Philadelphia / Cleared Out – 20 Dec 1720 – Count 1+					

	1722	*Principio*	Sloop		Benjamin	Haddock	Start	Philadelphia	[10 Mar 1722] [10 Mar 1722]	>	Principio Creek / Sasquehannah		
	M-H-012							[Pennsylvania]			Maryland		
	S-P-010												
							>	Philadelphia	[1 Nov 1722] [15 Nov 1722]	>	Maryland		
								[Pennsylvania]					
	7:28,126,132												

	1720 – 1723	*Priscilla & Merriam*	Ship		John	Richards	Start	Barbados		>	Philadelphia	18 Sept 1720 [31 Jan 1721] [21 Feb 1721]	
	M-R-008										[Pennsylvania]		
	S-P-011												
							>	Barbados		[>]	Milford Haven		
											[Wales]		
							>	Cork		>	Philadelphia	[23 Aug 1722] [30 Aug 1722] [11 Dec 1722]	
								[Ireland]			[Pennsylvania]		
							>	London		>	Downs		
								[England]			[England]		
							>	Philadelphia	[4 Oct 1723]				
								[Pennsylvania]					
	5:103 / 6:14,20 / 7:99,102,142 / 8:106							(Known Passengers / Quaker) Philadelphia / Inward – 23 Aug 1722 – Count 2+					

	1720	*Prosperity*	Ship		John	Brown	Start	Philadelphia	[14 Apr 1720] [14 Apr 1720]	>	Montrose		
	M-B-025							[Pennsylvania]			[Scotland]		
	S-P-012												
	5:36												

	1720	*Prosperous*	Sloop		Christopher	Smith	Start	Bermuda		>	Philadelphia	24 Oct 1720 [10 Nov 1720] [24 Nov 1720]	
	M-S-016										[Pennsylvania]		
	S-P-013												
							>	Barbados					
	5:120,126,133												

Group	Ship				Captain / Master		Passage	Arrival / Departure 1		Passage	Arrival / Departure 2		Page
	Year	Name	Type	Burden	First Name	Last Name	Length	Port	Arrival / Entered Inwards	Length	Port	Arrival / Entered Inwards	
R – S	MSTR ID#								Custom In / Entered Out			Custom In / Entered Out	30
	SHIP ID#	Registry Location						State / Country	Custom Out / Cleared Out		State / Country	Custom Out / Cleared Out	
									Departure			Departure	
	Source							Notes					

	Year / ID	Name	Type	Burden	First	Last	Length	Port / State	Dates		Port / State	Dates
	1721 M-L-006 S-R-001	Rainbow	Sloop		David	Lindsey	Start	[North Carolina]		>	Philadelphia [Pennsylvania]	30 May 1721 [8 Jun 1721]
							>	[North Carolina]				
	Source: 6:56,58											
	1723 M-J-003 S-R-002	Raven	Sloop		Matthew	Jenkins	Start	Rhode Island		>	Philadelphia [Pennsylvania]	[8 Aug 1723] [22 Aug 1723] [12 Sept 1723]
							>	Rhode Island				
	Source: 8:86,91,98											
	1723 M-H-013 S-R-003	Richard & Mary	Ship		Joseph	Hasell	Start	Bristol [England]		>	Philadelphia [Pennsylvania]	[13 Jun 1723] [4 Jul 1723]
							>	Virginia				
	Source: 8:66,70,73 — Notes: (Deserted Ship / Crew) Philadelphia / Docked - 27 Jun 1723 - Count 1											
	1719 – 1720 M-M-009 S-R-004	Royal George	Ship		Peter	Moore	Start	Philadelphia [Pennsylvania]	[29 Dec 1719] 18 Jan 1720	>	Madeira Island [Portugal]	
	Source: 5:4,12											
	1720 M-A-007 S-S-001	Samuel	Sloop		Abraham	Adderly	Start	Turks Island		>	Philadelphia [Pennsylvania]	[9 Jun 1720] [9 Jun 1720] [7 Jul 1720]
							>	Antigua				
	Source: 5:60,72											
	1722 M-H-014 S-S-002	Samuel & Mary	Sloop		Thomas	Handy	Start	Philadelphia [Pennsylvania]	[29 Nov 1722] [11 Dec 1722]	>	Bermuda	
	Source: 7:138,142											
	1723 M-P-007 S-S-003	Sarah	Scallop		William	Pattison	Start	Philadelphia [Pennsylvania]	[25 Jul 1723] [29 Jul 1723]	>	Bermuda	
	Source: 8:81,84											

Group	Ship				Captain / Master		Passage	Arrival / Departure 1		Passage	Arrival / Departure 2		Page
	Year	Name	Type	Burden	First Name	Last Name	Length	Port	Arrival / Entered Inwards; Custom In / Entered Out; Custom Out / Cleared Out; Departure	Length	Port	Arrival / Entered Inwards; Custom In / Entered Out; Custom Out / Cleared Out; Departure	
S	MSTR ID# / SHIP ID#	Registry Location						State / Country			State / Country		31
	Source							Notes					

Sarah & Mary

1720	Sarah & Mary	Sloop
M-N-003		
S-S-004		

Captain / Master: Samuel Northey
Passage Length: Start

Port		Passage	Port	Dates
North Carolina		>	Philadelphia [Pennsylvania]	28 Nov 1720 / [20 Dec 1720] / [27 Dec 1720]
> North Carolina				

Source: 5:136 / 6:2,4

Sea Flower

1721 – 1722	Sea Flower	Sloop
M-H-015		
S-S-005		

Captain / Master: Jehoshaphat Hollands
Passage Length: Start

Port	Date	Passage	Port
Philadelphia [Pennsylvania]	[9 Nov 1721]	>	North Carolina
> Philadelphia [Pennsylvania]	[5 Apr 1722]	[>]	North Carolina
> Philadelphia [Pennsylvania]	[1 Nov 1722]		

Source: 6:130 / 7:40,126

Sea Nymph

1721	Sea Nymph	Sloop
M-W-012		
S-S-006		

Captain / Master: John Williams
Passage Length: Start

Port	Passage	Port	Dates
South Carolina	>	Philadelphia [Pennsylvania]	[18 May 1721] / [1 Jun 1721] / [21 Jun 1721]
> Antigua			

Source: 6:49,56,63

Society

1721	Society	Sloop
M-T-007		
S-S-007		

Captain / Master: John Thornton
Passage Length: Start

Port	Passage	Port	Dates
Jamaica	>	Philadelphia [Pennsylvania]	[26 Oct 1721] / [27 Feb 1722] / [10 Mar 1722]
> Jamaica			

Source: 6:122 / 7:23,28

Speedwell

1721	Speedwell	Sloop
M-B-026		
S-S-008		

Captain / Master: John Barber
Passage Length: Start

Port	Passage	Port	Dates
Rhode Island	>	Philadelphia [Pennsylvania]	[30 Mar 1721] / [13 Apr 1721] / [20 Apr 1721]
> Rhode Island			

Source: 6:34,38,40

Group	Ship Year / MSTR ID# / SHIP ID#	Name / Registry Location	Type	Burden	Source	Captain First Name	Captain Last Name	Passage Length	A/D 1 Port / State-Country	Arrival-Entered Inwards / Custom In-Entered Out / Custom Out-Cleared Out / Departure	Passage Length	A/D 2 Port / State-Country	Dates / Notes	Page
S	1721 / M-V-004 / S-S-009	*Speedwell*	Sloop		6:100,104,108	John	Vesey	Start / >	Turks Island / Jamaica		>	Philadelphia / [Pennsylvania]	[7 Sept 1721] [14 Sept 1721] [28 Sept 1721]	32
S	1721 / M-C-006 / S-S-010	*Speedwell*	Sloop		6:108,112	James	Cahoone	Start / >	Salem [New Jersey] / Salem [New Jersey]		>	Philadelphia / [Pennsylvania]	[28 Sept 1721] [28 Sept 1721] [5 Oct 1721]	32
S	1722 / M-W-013 / S-S-011	*Speedwell*	Sloop		7:94,96,106	David	Whitney	Start / >	Turks Island / Jamaica		>	Philadelphia / [Pennsylvania]	[9 Aug 1722] [16 Aug 1722] [6 Sept 1722]	32
S	1723 / M-B-027 / S-S-012	*Speedwell*	Sloop		8:73	William	Bell	>	Philadelphia / [Pennsylvania]	[4 Jul 1723]	>	Barbados		32
S	1721 / M-T-008 / S-S-013	*Sperma Caeti*	Sloop		6:60,67	Joshua	Thomas	Start / >	Boston [Massachusetts] / Newfoundland		>	Philadelphia / [Pennsylvania]	[15 Jun 1721] [15 Jun 1721] [29 Jun 1721]	32
S	1721 / M-R-009 / S-S-014	*Starling*	Ship		6:130,138	Parker	Roe	Start / >	Milford Haven [Wales] / Milford Haven [Wales]		>	Philadelphia / [Pennsylvania]	[9 Nov 1721] [30 Nov 1721]	32

Group	Ship				Captain / Master		Passage	Arrival / Departure 1		Passage	Arrival / Departure 2		Page
	Year	Name	Type	Burden	First Name	Last Name	Length	Port	Arrival / Entered Inwards / Custom In / Entered Out	Length	Port	Arrival / Entered Inwards / Custom In / Entered Out	
S	MSTR ID#	Registry Location						State / Country	Custom Out / Cleared Out / Departure		State / Country	Custom Out / Cleared Out / Departure	33
	SHIP ID#												
	Source							Notes					

1720	Susanna	Sloop		Thomas	Parham	Start			>	Philadelphia	[12 May 1720]
M-P-008							Virginia			[Pennsylvania]	[19 May 1720]
S-S-015						>					
							Virginia				

5:50,53

1719 – 1720	Swallow	Schooner		Joseph	Gorham	Start	Boston	[? Dec 1719] / [? Dec 1719]	>		[18 Dec 1719]
M-G-009							[Massachusetts]			Rhode Island	
S-S-016						>	New London	[8 Mar 1720]	>		[11 Mar 1720]
							[Connecticut]			Rhode Island	
						>	Boston	[? Mar 1720] / [28 Mar 1720]	>	Newport	
							[Massachusetts]			[Rhode Island]	
						>					
							[Connecticut]				

NO SUPPORTING DATA TO LINK TIMELINE

1722 – 1723						Start	Boston	[16 Apr 1722]	>	Newport	
S-S-016							[Massachusetts]			[Rhode Island]	
						>			>	Boston	[25 Jun 1722]
							Connecticut			[Massachusetts]	[9 Jul 1722]
						>			>	Boston	[10 Sept 1722]
							Connecticut			[Massachusetts]	[24 Sept 1722]
						>			>	Philadelphia	[18 Oct 1722] / [18 Oct 1722] / [25 Oct 1722]
							Connecticut			[Pennsylvania]	
						>	Boston		[>]	Connecticut	
							[Massachusetts]				
						>	Boston	[25 Mar 1723] / [1 Apr 1723] / [8 Apr 1723]	>	Connecticut	
							[Massachusetts]				
						>	Boston	[10 Jun 1723] / [15 Jun 1723] / [29 Jun 1723]	>	Connecticut	
							[Massachusetts]				
						>	Boston	[31 Aug 1723]	>	Connecticut	
							[Massachusetts]	[21 Sept 1723]			

5:2,4,10,32,34,36 / 7:120,122 / 20:37,47,49,58,60,86,87,88,97,98,100,109,111,112

Group	Ship				Captain / Master		Passage	Arrival / Departure 1		Passage	Arrival / Departure 2		Page
	Year	Name	Type	Burden	First Name	Last Name	Length	Port	Arrival / Entered Inwards	Length	Port	Arrival / Entered Inwards	
S – T	MSTR ID#								Custom In / Entered Out			Custom In / Entered Out	34
	SHIP ID#	Registry Location						State / Country	Custom Out / Cleared Out		State / Country	Custom Out / Cleared Out	
									Departure			Departure	
	Source						Notes						

1723	Syzeragh / Sizergh	Ship			Jeremiah	Cowman	Start	White Haven		>	Dublin		
M-C-007								[England]			[Ireland]		
S-S-017							>	Philadelphia	[26 Feb 1723]	>	Lancaster		
								[Pennsylvania]	[9 May 1723]		[England]		
	8:24,50												

1722	Thomas & Sarah	Sloop			Samuel	Emmes	Start	Boston		>	Philadelphia	[18 Oct 1722]	
M-E-002								[Massachusetts]			[Pennsylvania]	[18 Oct 1722]	
S-T-001							>	Christiana					
								[Delaware]					
	7:120												

1720 – 1723	Trine Hope	Ship			Warner	Holt	Start	London		>	Philadelphia	[7 Apr 1720]
M-H-016												[21 Apr 1720]
S-T-002								[England]			[Pennsylvania]	[26 May 1720]
							>	Antigua				
							NO SUPPORTING DATA TO LINK TIMELINE					
							Start	Isle of May		>	Philadelphia	[25 May 1721]
												[6 Jul 1721]
								[Scotland]			[Pennsylvania]	[3 Aug 1721]
							>	Barbados		>	Philadelphia	[9 Nov 1721]
												[30 Nov 1721]
											[Pennsylvania]	[19 Apr 1722]
							>	Barbados				
							NO SUPPORTING DATA TO LINK TIMELINE					
							Start			>	Philadelphia	[4 Jul 1723]
												[4 Jul 1723]
								Maryland			[Pennsylvania]	[15 Aug 1723]
							>	?? ??? 1723 – Cut away Main & Mizzen Masts		&	Ships Crew & Ship Saved	
								Violent Storm 20 Leagues from Bermuda			Ship bound for Antigua forced back to Refit	
							>	Philadelphia	18 Sept 1723			
								[Pennsylvania]				
	5:34,38,56 / 6:53,71,87,130,138 / 7:46 / 8:73,88,100												

Group		Ship				Captain / Master		Passage	Arrival / Departure 1		Passage	Arrival / Departure 2		Page
	Year	Name	Type	Burden	First Name	Last Name	Length	Port	Arrival / Entered Inwards / Custom In / Entered Out / Custom Out / Cleared Out / Departure	Length	Port	Arrival / Entered Inwards / Custom In / Entered Out / Custom Out / Cleared Out / Departure	
W	MSTR ID# / SHIP ID#	Registry Location						State / Country			State / Country		35
		Source							Notes				

Row 1 — 1720–1722, M-C-008, S-W-001, William, Sloop — Samuel Cooper

Passage	Port	Dates	Passage	Port	Dates
Start	Bermuda		>	Philadelphia / [Pennsylvania]	23 Oct 1720 / [3 Nov 1720] / [24 Nov 1720]
>	Montserrat		[>]	St Christopher's	
>	Anguilla		>	Philadelphia / [Pennsylvania]	[4 May 1721] / [25 May 1721]
>	Bermuda		>	Philadelphia / [Pennsylvania]	[2 Nov 1721] / [9 Nov 1721] / [7 Dec 1721]
>	Barbados		[>]	Bermuda	
>	New York / [New York]	[30 Apr 1722] / [21 May 1722]	>	Curacao	
[>]	New York / [New York]	[11 Nov 1722] / [3 Dec 1722]	>	Barbados	

Source: 5:120,123,133 / 6:42,44,53,125,130,140 / 7:51,60,132,144

Row 2 — 1720, M-H-017, S-W-002, William, Sloop — Thomas Hurst

Passage	Port	Passage	Port	Dates
Start	Jamaica	>	Philadelphia / [Pennsylvania]	14 Sept 1720 / [24 Nov 1720] / [13 Dec 1720]
>	Curacao			

Source: 5:99,133,141

Row 3 — 1720, M-S-017, S-W-003, William, Sloop — Edward Styles

Passage	Port	Passage	Port	Dates
Start	Montserrat	>	Philadelphia / [Pennsylvania]	15 Sept 1720 / [13 Oct 1720]
>	Barbados			

Source: 5:99,112

Row 4 — 1720, M-J-004, S-W-004, William, Sloop — Thomas Joel

Passage	Port	Passage	Port	Dates
Start	Bermuda	>	Philadelphia / [Pennsylvania]	27 Aug 1720 / [8 Sept 1720] / [29 Sept 1720]
>	Barbados			

Source: 5:94,96,107

Group	Ship				Captain / Master		Passage	Arrival / Departure 1		Passage	Arrival / Departure 2		Page
	Year	Name	Type	Burden	First Name	Last Name	Length	Port	Arrival / Entered Inwards	Length	Port	Arrival / Entered Inwards	
W	MSTR ID#								Custom In / Entered Out			Custom In / Entered Out	36
	SHIP ID#	Registry Location						State / Country	Custom Out / Cleared Out		State / Country	Custom Out / Cleared Out	
									Departure			Departure	
	Source							Notes					

1721	William	Sloop		George	Fraser	Start	Philadelphia	[23 Mar 1721]	>	Boston		
M-F-006								[30 Mar 1721]				
S-W-005							[Pennsylvania]			[Massachusetts]		
						[>]			>	Philadelphia	[18 May 1721]	
											[25 May 1721]	
							Virginia			[Pennsylvania]	[8 Jun 1721]	
						>	Amboy					
							[New Jersey]					
6:32,34,49,53,58												

1722	William	Sloop		Benjamin	Tucker	Start	Anguilla		>	Philadelphia	[26 Apr 1722]	
M-T-009											[10 May 1722]	
S-W-006										[Pennsylvania]	[31 May 1722]	
						>	Bermuda					
7:48,54,64												

1721	William & Mary	Brigantine		Nicholas	Sylvan	Start	Bristol		13 Weeks	Philadelphia	[7 Sept 1721]	
M-S-018											[19 Oct 1721]	
S-W-007							[England]	[? Jun 1721]		[Pennsylvania]	[23 Nov 1721]	
						>	Bristol					
							[England]					
6:100,120,134												

1720	William & Mary	Sloop		William	Peer	Start	North Carolina		>	Philadelphia	20 Apr 1720	
M-P-009											[9 Jun 1720]	
S-W-008										[Pennsylvania]	[16 Jun 1720]	
						>	North Carolina					
5:38,41,60,63												

Group	Year / MSTR ID# / SHIP ID#	Name	Type	Burden	First Name	Last Name	Length	Port / State-Country	Arr/Cust In/Cust Out/Dep	Length	Port / State-Country	Arr/Cust In/Cust Out/Dep	Page
Multi			Ship		Captain / Master		Passage	Arrival / Departure 1		Passage	Arrival / Departure 2		**37**

Record 1

Year	Name	Type	Burden	First Name	Last Name	Length	Port / State·Country	Dates	Length	Port / State·Country	Dates
1721 – 1722	*Dolphin*	Sloop		William	Rush	Start	Philadelphia [Pennsylvania]	[10 Aug 1721]	>	Patuxent [Maryland]	
M-R-010											
S-D-007						>	Potomac [Maryland]		>	Philadelphia [Pennsylvania]	[7 Sept 1721] [30 Nov 1721] [7 Dec 1721]
						>	Potomac [Maryland]		>	Accomack Virginia	
						>	Philadelphia [Pennsylvania]	[6 Feb 1722] [20 Feb 1722]	>	Accomack Virginia	
						>	Philadelphia [Pennsylvania]	[29 Mar 1722]			

XXXXXXXXXX XXXXXXXXXX Captain / Master Changed Ships XXXXXXXXXX XXXXXXXXXX

| 1723 | | | | | | Start | Philadelphia [Pennsylvania] | | > | Boston [Massachusetts] | [4 May 1723] |
| S-?-013 | | | | | | | | | | | |

Source: 6:90,100,138,140 / 7:13,20,38 / 20:92

Record 2

Year	Name	Type	Burden	First Name	Last Name	Length	Port / State·Country	Dates	Length	Port / State·Country	Dates
1719 – 1721	*Dolphin*	Sloop		Robert	Palmer	Start	Philadelphia [Pennsylvania]	[22 Dec 1719]	>	Jamaica	
M-P-010											
S-D-008						>	Philadelphia [Pennsylvania]	18 May 1720 [9 Jun 1720] [14 Jul 1720]	>	Jamaica	
						>	Philadelphia [Pennsylvania]	23 Nov 1720 [7 Feb 1721] [2 Mar 1721]	>	Barbados	

XXXXXXXXXX XXXXXXXXXX Captain / Master Changed Ships XXXXXXXXXX XXXXXXXXXX

| 1722 | *Susanna* | Ship | | | | Start | Philadelphia [Pennsylvania] | [5 Apr 1722] [14 Jun 1722] | > | South Carolina | |
| S-S-018 | | | | | | | | | | | |

XXXXXXXXXX XXXXXXXXXX Captain / Master Changed Ships XXXXXXXXXX XXXXXXXXXX

| 1723 | *Carolina Packet* | Ship | | | | Start | South Carolina | | > | Philadelphia [Pennsylvania] | [11 Oct 1723] [14 Nov 1723] [29 Nov 1723] |
| S-C-011 | | | | | | > | South Carolina | | | | |

Source: 5:2,53,56,60,75,133 / 6:16,23 / 7:40,70 / 8:109,126,130

Group	Ship				Captain / Master		Passage	Arrival / Departure 1		Passage	Arrival / Departure 2		Page
Multi	Year	Name	Type	Burden	First Name	Last Name	Length	Port	Arrival / Entered Inwards / Custom In / Entered Out	Length	Port	Arrival / Entered Inwards / Custom In / Entered Out	38
	MSTR ID#	Registry Location						State / Country	Custom Out / Cleared Out / Departure		State / Country	Custom Out / Cleared Out / Departure	
	SHIP ID#												
	Source							Notes					

Year / ID	Name	Type	First Name	Last Name	Length	Port / State	Arr/Dep 1	Length	Port / State	Arr/Dep 2
1720 M-C-009 S-L-006	Laurel	Ship	John	Coppel	Start	Liverpool [England]		>	Cork [Ireland]	
					>	Philadelphia [Pennsylvania]	30 Aug 1720 [15 Sept 1720] [15 Sept 1720]	>	Maryland	

XXXXXXXXXX XXXXXXXXXX Captain / Master Changed Ships XXXXXXXXXX XXXXXXXXXX

Year / ID	Name	Type	First Name	Last Name	Length	Port / State	Arr/Dep 1	Length	Port / State	Arr/Dep 2
1722 S-G-005	Greyhound	Ship			Start	Port Royal Jamaica	28 Aug 1722 Drove on Dry Land	&	Nothing Saved Ship & Ships Crew Were Lost	
					>	Port Royal Jamaica	Lost In Harbor / Hurricane			

Source	Notes
5:94,99 / 7:146	(Known Passengers / Palatine) Philadelphia / Inward – 30 Aug 1720 – Count 340+

Year / ID	Name	Type	First Name	Last Name	Length	Port / State	Arr/Dep 1	Length	Port / State	Arr/Dep 2
1720 M-G-010 S-B-013	Bedminster	Ship	James	Gordon	Start	Bristol [England]		11 Weeks & 3 Days	Philadelphia [Pennsylvania]	18 Jun 1720 [7 Jul 1720] [14 Jul 1720]
					>	South Carolina				

XXXXXXXXXX XXXXXXXXXX Captain / Master Changed Ships XXXXXXXXXX XXXXXXXXXX

Year / ID	Name	Type	First Name	Last Name	Length	Port / State	Arr/Dep 1	Length	Port / State	Arr/Dep 2
1721 – 1722 S-P-014	Pennsylvania Merchant	Ship			Start	Bristol [England]	3 Apr 1721	>	Philadelphia [Pennsylvania]	26 Jun 1721 [17 Aug 1721] [26 Oct 1721]
					>	Bristol [England]		>	Philadelphia [Pennsylvania]	[17 May 1722] [24 May 1722] [28 Jun 1722]
					>	Port Royal Jamaica	28 Aug 1722 Drove on Shore	&	Ships Crew Saved Ship Was Lost	
					>	Port Royal Jamaica	Lost In Harbor / Hurricane			

XXXXXXXXXX XXXXXXXXXX Captain / Master Changed Ships XXXXXXXXXX XXXXXXXXXX

Year / ID	Name	Type	First Name	Last Name	Length	Port / State	Arr/Dep 1	Length	Port / State	Arr/Dep 2
1723 S-E-008	Elizabeth	Sloop			Start	New York [New York]	[10 Jun 1723]	>	Bristol [England]	

Source	Notes
5:67,72,75 / 6:60,67,92,122 / 7:58,60,76,146 / 8:62,65	

Group	Year	Name	Type	Burden	First Name	Last Name	Length	Port / State/Country	Arrival/Entered Inwards, Custom In/Entered Out, Custom Out/Cleared Out, Departure	Length	Port / State/Country	Arrival/Entered Inwards, Custom In/Entered Out, Custom Out/Cleared Out, Departure	Page
Multi													39

Ship				
Year	Name	Type	Burden	
MSTR ID#	Registry Location			
SHIP ID#				
Source				

Row 1

Year: 1720	Name: *William*	Type: Sloop	Burden:	First Name: William	Last Name: Spafford	Length: Start	Port: Antigua		Length: >	Port: Philadelphia / [Pennsylvania]	[1 Jun 1720] / [9 Jun 1720] / [16 Jun 1720]
MSTR ID#: MS-019											
SHIP ID#: S-W-009											
						>	Antigua		>	Philadelphia / [Pennsylvania]	7 Oct 1720

XXXXXXXXX XXXXXXXXX Captain / Master Changed Ships XXXXXXXXX XXXXXXXXX

Row 2

Year	Name	Type	Burden	Port 1	Dates 1	Length 2	Port 2	Dates 2
1721 - 1723	*Sarah*	Sloop	22 Tons	Philadelphia [Pennsylvania] — Start	[27 Apr 1721] / [18 May 1721]	>	Antigua	
S-S-019	Philadelphia, Pennsylvania			Philadelphia [Pennsylvania] — >	16 Aug 1721 / [7 Sept 1721]	>	Virginia	
				Philadelphia [Pennsylvania] — >	16 Nov 1721 / [30 Nov 1721] / [6 Feb 1722]	>	Barbados	
				Philadelphia [Pennsylvania] — >	10 May 1722 / [21 Jun 1722] / [19 Jul 1722]	>	Barbados	
				Philadelphia [Pennsylvania] — >	[1 Nov 1722] / [8 Nov 1722] / [29 Nov 1722]	>	Madeira Island [Portugal]	
				Barbados — [>]		>	Philadelphia [Pennsylvania]	[20 Jun 1723] / [1 Jul 1723] / [11 Jul 1723]
				Jamaica — >		>	Philadelphia [Pennsylvania]	[24 Oct 1723] / [31 Oct 1723] / [21 Nov 1723]
				Jamaica — >				

Source: 3:115 / 5:58,60,63,112 / 6:42,49,92,100,132,134,138 / 7:13,54,74,85,126,130,138 / 8:68,73,76,114,118,128

Notes: (Sloop / Sarah) Philadelphia / Registered – 20 Apr 1721

Row 3

Year: 1720	Name: *Traveler*	Type: Sloop	Burden:	First Name: Samuel	Last Name: Moale	Length: Start	Port: Antigua		Length: >	Port: Boston / [Massachusetts]	[4 Jan 1720] / [18 Jan 1720]
M-M-010											
S-T-003						>	Leeward Islands				

XXXXXXXXX XXXXXXXXX Captain / Master Changed Ships XXXXXXXXX XXXXXXXXX

Row 4

Year: 1720	Name: *Post Boy*	Type: Sloop	Burden:	Length: Start	Port: Antigua		Length: >	Port: Philadelphia / [Pennsylvania]	[19 May 1720] / [23 Jun 1720]
				>	Antigua				
S-P-015									

Source: 5:14,18,53,58,67

Group	Ship				Captain / Master		Passage	Arrival / Departure 1		Passage	Arrival / Departure 2		Page
Multi	Year	Name	Type	Burden	First Name	Last Name	Length	Port	Arrival / Entered Inwards	Length	Port	Arrival / Entered Inwards	40
	MSTR ID#								Custom In / Entered Out			Custom In / Entered Out	
	SHIP ID#	Registry Location						State / Country	Custom Out / Cleared Out		State / Country	Custom Out / Cleared Out	
	Source								Departure		Notes	Departure	

Year	Name	Type	Burden	First Name	Last Name	Length	Port	A/D1 dates	Length	Port	A/D2 dates
1720 – 1721	*Hannah*	Sloop		Henry	Combs	Start	Philadelphia	[31 Mar 1720]	>	Newfoundland	
M-C-010								[12 May 1720]			
S-H-009							[Pennsylvania]				
						[>]	London		>	English Channel	[? Nov 1720]
							[England]				
						>	Barbados		>	Philadelphia	[30 Mar 1721]
											[11 May 1721]
										[Pennsylvania]	[25 May 1721]
						>	Newfoundland				

XXXXXXXXX XXXXXXXXXX Captain / Master Changed Ships XXXXXXXXX XXXXXXXXXX

Year	Name	Type	Burden	First Name	Last Name	Length	Port	A/D1 dates	Length	Port	A/D2 dates
1722	*Charles*	Sloop				Start	Philadelphia	[12 Apr 1722]	>	Port Royal	28 Aug 1722
								[17 May 1722]			
S-C-012	Philadelphia, Pennsylvania						[Pennsylvania]			Jamaica	Lost
						&	Captain, Mate & 1 Man Lost		&	2 Men & Boy Saved	
							Ship Was Lost			Taken To New York On Board	
										(Sloop / Jolly) (Captain John Tickle)	
						>	Port Royal	Lost In Harbor / Hurricane			
							Jamaica				

5:32,50 / 6:6,18,34,46,53 / 7:42,58,144

Year	Name	Type	Burden	First Name	Last Name	Length	Port	A/D1 dates	Length	Port	A/D2 dates
1720	*Hannah*	Ship		John	Annis Jr	Start	Philadelphia		35 Days	London	Arrived Before
M-A-008											[27 Jan 1720]
S-H-010							[Pennsylvania]			[England]	

XXXXXXXXX XXXXXXXXXX Captain / Master Changed Ships XXXXXXXXX XXXXXXXXXX

Year	Name	Type	Burden	First Name	Last Name	Length	Port	A/D1 dates	Length	Port	A/D2 dates
1721 – 1723	*Sarah*	Ship				Start	Philadelphia	[27 Jul 1721]	>	Jamaica	
								[26 Oct 1721]			
S-S-020							[Pennsylvania]				
						[>]	London		>	Philadelphia	[15 Nov 1722]
											[29 Nov 1722]
							[England]			[Pennsylvania]	[19 Feb 1723]
						>	Jamaica		>	London	
										[England]	
						[>]	Bay of Honduras		>	Philadelphia	[14 Nov 1723]
										[Pennsylvania]	

5:36 / 6:84,122 / 7:132,138 / 8:18,50,126

Group	Ship				Captain / Master		Passage	Arrival / Departure 1		Passage	Arrival / Departure 2		Page
	Year	Name	Type	Burden	First Name	Last Name	Length	Port	Arrival / Entered Inwards	Length	Port	Arrival / Entered Inwards	
Multi									Custom In / Entered Out			Custom In / Entered Out	41
	MSTR ID#							State / Country	Custom Out / Cleared Out		State / Country	Custom Out / Cleared Out	
	SHIP ID#	Registry Location							Departure			Departure	
		Source								Notes			

	Year	Name	Type	Burden	First Name	Last Name	Length	Port	A/D 1 dates	Length	Port	A/D 2 dates
	1720	*Concord*	Sloop		John	Dickinson	Start		[9 Jan 1720]	>	Barbados	
	M-D-005							Rhode Island				
	S-C-013											

XXXXXXXXXX XXXXXXXXXX Captain / Master Changed Ships XXXXXXXXXX XXXXXXXXXX

	Year	Name	Type	Length	Port	A/D 1 dates	Length	Port	A/D 2 dates
	1720 – 1721	*Deborah*	Sloop	Start	Bermuda		>	Philadelphia	[7 Apr 1720] / [21 Apr 1720] / [12 May 1720]
	S-D-009							[Pennsylvania]	
				>	Bermuda		>	Turks Island	
				>	New York / [New York]	16 Oct 1720 / [31 Oct 1720] / [14 Nov 1720]	>	Barbados	
				[>]	Bermuda / [Pennsylvania]		>	Philadelphia	[13 Apr 1721] / [27 Apr 1721] / [11 May 1721]
				>	Jamaica / [Pennsylvania]		>	Philadelphia	20 Aug 1721 / [31 Aug 1721] / [28 Sept 1721]
				>	Jamaica				

NO SUPPORTING DATA TO LINK TIMELINE

	1723	*Deborah*	Sloop	Start	Bermuda / [New York]		>	New York	15 Sept 1723 / [23 Sept 1723]
	S-D-009			>	Jamaica				

5:18,34,38,50,115,123,129 / 6:38,42,46,94,96,108 / 8:100,106

	Year	Name	Type	First Name	Last Name	Length	Port	A/D 1 dates	Length	Port	A/D 2 dates
	1722	*Abigail*	Brigantine	Samuel	Hillary	Start			>	Philadelphia	[12 Jul 1722] / XXXXXXXXXXXXXX / XXXXXXXXXXXXXX
	M-H-025						Rhode Island			[Pennsylvania]	XXXXXXXXXXXXXX
	S-A-011										

XXXXXXXXXX XXXXXXXXXX Captain / Master Changed Ships XXXXXXXXXX XXXXXXXXXX

	1722	*Endeavor*	Brigantine			Start	Philadelphia / [Pennsylvania]	XXXXXXXXXXXXXX / XXXXXXXXXXXXXX / [11 Dec 1722]	>	Christiana / [Delaware]	
	S-E-013										

7:82,142

Group	Year / MSTR ID# / SHIP ID#	Ship Name	Type	Burden	First Name	Last Name	Passage Length	Port / State/Country	Arrival/Entered Inwards · Custom In/Entered Out · Custom Out/Cleared Out · Departure	Passage Length	Port / State/Country	Arrival/Departure 2
Multi	1720 / M-C-001 / S-M-022	Mary Hope	Sloop		John	Cassly / Casely	Start	Philadelphia [Pennsylvania]	[6 Oct 1720] · [13 Oct 1720]	>	Virginia	
							>	Philadelphia [Pennsylvania]	28 Nov 1720 · XXXXXXXXXXXXXX · XXXXXXXXXXXXXX · XXXXXXXXXXXXXX			

NO SUPPORTING DATA TO LINK TIMELINE

	Year / SHIP ID#	Ship Name	Type		First Name	Last Name	Passage	Port / State/Country	Dates	Passage	Port / State/Country	Dates
	1723 / S-M-023	Mary Hope	Scallop				Start	Philadelphia [Pennsylvania]	[26 Sept 1723]	>	New York [New York]	[21 Oct 1723] · [21 Oct 1723]
							>	Philadelphia [Pennsylvania]				

Source: 5:110,112,136 / 8:103,114

Group	Year / MSTR ID# / SHIP ID#	Ship Name	Type		First Name	Last Name	Passage	Port / State/Country	Dates	Passage	Port / State/Country	Dates
	1722 / M-S-020 / S-?-014		Sloop		Jonathan	Swain	Start	Cape May [New Jersey]		>	Philadelphia [Pennsylvania]	22 Jul 1722

XXXXXXXXXX XXXXXXXXXX Captain / Master Changed Ships XXXXXXXXXX XXXXXXXXXX

| | 1724 / S-T-004 | Two Brothers | Sloop | | | | Start | [Philadelphia] [Pennsylvania] | | > | | |

Source: 3:228,240 / 7:85

Group	Year / MSTR ID# / SHIP ID#	Ship Name	Type		First Name	Last Name	Passage	Port / State/Country	Dates	Passage	Port / State/Country	Dates
	1721 / M-O-001 / S-M-024	Mary Hope	Sloop		John	Oliver	Start	Philadelphia [Pennsylvania]	XXXXXXXXXXXXXX · [3 Aug 1721] · [17 Aug 1721]	>	Virginia	
							>	Philadelphia [Pennsylvania]	[19 Oct 1721] · XXXXXXXXXXXXXX · XXXXXXXXXXXXXX · XXXXXXXXXXXXXX			

XXXXXXXXXX XXXXXXXXXX Captain / Master Changed Ships XXXXXXXXXX XXXXXXXXXX

	1721 – 1722 / S-G-006	Grace & Elizabeth	Sloop				Start	Philadelphia [Pennsylvania]	XXXXXXXXXXXXXX · XXXXXXXXXXXXXX · [30 Nov 1721]	>	North Carolina	
							>	Philadelphia [Pennsylvania]	[22 Mar 1722] · [5 Apr 1722] · [12 Apr 1722]	>	North Carolina	
							>	Philadelphia [Pennsylvania]	[21 Jun 1722] · [5 Jul 1722] · [12 Jul 1722]	>	North Carolina	
							>	Philadelphia [Pennsylvania]	[6 Sept 1722] · [13 Sept 1722]	>	North Carolina	
							>	Philadelphia [Pennsylvania]	[15 Nov 1722] · [29 Nov 1722] · [29 Nov 1722]	>	Boston [Massachusetts]	

Source: 6:87,92,120,138 / 7:34,40,42,74,79,82,106,108,132,138

Group	Ship				Captain / Master		Passage	Arrival / Departure 1		Passage	Arrival / Departure 2		Page
	Year	Name	Type	Burden	First Name	Last Name	Length	Port	Arrival / Entered Inwards / Custom In / Entered Out	Length	Port	Arrival / Entered Inwards / Custom In / Entered Out	
Multi	MSTR ID#	Registry Location						State / Country	Custom Out / Cleared Out / Departure		State / Country	Custom Out / Cleared Out / Departure	43
	SHIP ID#												
	Source							Notes					

1721	Jane	Sloop		William	Whither	Start	Barbados		>	Philadelphia	[25 May 1721] / [1 Jun 1721]
M-W-014										[Pennsylvania]	[29 Jun 1721]
						>	Madeira Island				
							[Portugal]				

XXXXXXXXXX XXXXXXXXXX Captain / Master Changed Ships XXXXXXXXXX XXXXXXXXXX

1722 – 1723	Vine	Sloop				Start	Philadelphia	XXXXXXXXXXXXXX / [16 Aug 1722] / [27 Sept 1722]	>	Barbados	
S-V-001							[Pennsylvania]				
						>	Philadelphia	[9 May 1723] / [6 Jun 1723] / [11 Jul 1723]	>	Barbados	
							[Pennsylvania]				
						>	Philadelphia	[21 Nov 1723]			
							[Pennsylvania]				

6:53,56,67 / 7:96,112 / 8:50,62,76,128

1719 – 1720	Mary	Sloop		Nathaniel	Owen	Start	Jamaica		>	New York	6 Dec 1719
M-O-002										[New York]	
S-M-025						>	Prime Hook	[8 Jan 1720]	>	Philadelphia	22 Jan 1720 / [17 Mar 1720] / [28 Apr 1720]
							Delaware			[Pennsylvania]	
						>	Jamaica				

XXXXXXXXXX XXXXXXXXXX Captain / Master Changed Ships XXXXXXXXXX XXXXXXXXXX

| 1720 | Clemmel | Sloop | | | | Start | Philadelphia | [24 Nov 1720] / [27 Dec 1720] | > | Jamaica | XXXXXXXXXXXXXX / XXXXXXXXXXXXXX / XXXXXXXXXXXXXX |
| S-C-014 | | | | | | | [Pennsylvania] | | | | |

XXXXXXXXXX XXXXXXXXXX Captain / Master Changed Ships XXXXXXXXXX XXXXXXXXXX

1721 – 1722	Three Williams	Sloop				Start	Jamaica	XXXXXXXXXXXXXX	>	Philadelphia	7 Aug 1721 / [21 Sept 1721] / [9 Nov 1721]
S-T-005										[Pennsylvania]	
						>	Jamaica				

NO SUPPORTING DATA TO LINK TIMELINE

						Start	Jamaica		>	Philadelphia	[6 Sept 1722] / [1 Nov 1722] / [15 Nov 1722]
										[Pennsylvania]	
						>	Virginia				

5:2,8,12,27,41,133 / 6:4,90,106,130 / 7:106,126,132

Group	Ship				Captain / Master		Passage	Arrival / Departure 1		Passage	Arrival / Departure 2		Page
	Year	Name	Type	Burden	First Name	Last Name	Length	Port	Arrival / Entered Inwards / Custom In / Entered Out	Length	Port	Arrival / Entered Inwards / Custom In / Entered Out	
Multi	MSTR ID#								Custom Out / Cleared Out			Custom Out / Cleared Out	44
	SHIP ID#	Registry Location						State / Country	Departure		State / Country	Departure	
	Source							Notes					

	Year	Name	Type	Burden	First Name	Last Name	Length	Port	A/D1	Length	Port	A/D2
	1719 – 1720	*Samuel & Sarah*	Sloop		Matthew	Phillips	Start	Providence		>	Philadelphia	[22 Dec 1719]
	M-P-011										[Pennsylvania]	18 Jan 1720
	S-S-021											
							>	?	Before 14 Apr 1720 / Taken / Pirates	>	Barbados	Never Reached Port / Taken / Pirates
							>	Santa Cruz / [Spain]		>	Winter Harbor / [Maine]	
							>	Philadelphia / [Pennsylvania]	Never Reached Port / Distress of Weather	>	Cape Porpoise / [Maine]	?? ??? 1720 / Seized – Taken to Boston
							>	Boston / [Massachusetts]				
								NO SUPPORTING DATA TO LINK TIMELINE				
							Start	Philadelphia / [Pennsylvania]	[3 Nov 1720] XXXXXXXXXXXXXX XXXXXXXXXXXXXX	>	Madeira Island / [Portugal]	Never Left For Port / See Next Ship Or Captain
					XXXXXXXXXX XXXXXXXXXX Captain / Master Changed Ships XXXXXXXXXX XXXXXXXXXX							
	1720	*Jane*	Sloop				Start	Philadelphia / [Pennsylvania]	XXXXXXXXXXXXXX XXXXXXXXXXXXXX [24 Nov 1720]	>	Madeira Island / [Portugal]	
	S-J-011											
	5:2,12,36,46,123,133											

	Year	Name	Type	Burden	First Name	Last Name	Length	Port	A/D1	Length	Port	A/D2
	1719 – 1720		Sloop		George	King	Start	Philadelphia / [Pennsylvania]	[22 Dec 1719]	>	Madeira Island / [Portugal]	
	M-K-002											
	S-?-015											
							>	Jamaica	Never Reached Port / Taken / Spanish Privateer	>	Porto Rico	10 Apr 1720 / Carried Into This Port
							>	St Thomas / [Virgin Islands]	13 May 1720 / Released As Prisoner			
					XXXXXXXXXX XXXXXXXXXX Captain / Master Changed Ships XXXXXXXXXX XXXXXXXXXX							
	1720 – 1721	*Vine*	Sloop				Start	Philadelphia / [Pennsylvania]	[6 Oct 1720] / [17 Nov 1720]	>	Madeira Island / [Portugal]	
	S-V-002											
							[>]	Barbados		>	Philadelphia / [Pennsylvania]	7 Dec 1721
	5:2,70,110,129 / 6:140											

Interact 1 — Page 45

Ship (Year / Name / Type / Burden / MSTR ID# / SHIP ID# / Registry Location / Source)	Captain / Master	Passage (Length)	Arrival / Departure 1 (Port / State·Country)	Arr/Entered Inwards · Custom In/Entered Out · Custom Out/Cleared Out · Departure	Passage (Length)	Arrival / Departure 2 (Port / State·Country)	Arr/Entered Inwards · Custom In/Entered Out · Custom Out/Cleared Out · Departure
1721 — George — Sloop — M-D-006 — S-G-007	John Darrell	Start	Jamaica		>	Philadelphia [Pennsylvania]	23 Jun 1721 / [6 Jul 1721] / [13 Jul 1721]
		>	Jamaica	XXXXXXXXXXXXXX / XXXXXXXXXXXXXX / XXXXXXXXXXXXXX			→ M-B-028 / S-G-007 / Page # 45
Source: 6:67,71,76							

1722 — George — Sloop — M-B-028 — S-G-007	John Burch	Start	Jamaica	XXXXXXXXXXXXXX	>	Philadelphia [Pennsylvania]	[12 Apr 1722] / [12 Apr 1722]
← M-D-006 / S-G-007 / Page # 45		>	Jamaica				
Source: 7:42							

Interact 2 — Page 45

Ship (Year / Name / Type / Burden / MSTR ID# / SHIP ID# / Registry Location / Source)	Captain / Master	Passage (Length)	Arrival / Departure 1 (Port / State·Country)	Arr/Entered Inwards · Custom In/Entered Out · Custom Out/Cleared Out · Departure	Passage (Length)	Arrival / Departure 2 (Port / State·Country)	Arr/Entered Inwards · Custom In/Entered Out · Custom Out/Cleared Out · Departure
1721 – 1722 — Hudson Galley — Ship — M-H-018 — S-H-011	Samuel Hollyman	Start	Philadelphia [Pennsylvania]	[20 Jul 1721] / [19 Oct 1721]	>	London [England]	
		>	Philadelphia [Pennsylvania]	[7 Jun 1722] / [21 Jun 1722] / [19 Jul 1722]	>	Antigua	XXXXXXXXXXXXXX / XXXXXXXXXXXXXX / XXXXXXXXXXXXXX → M-L-007 / S-H-011 / Page # 45
Source: 6:79,120 / 7:67,74,85							

1722 – 1723 — Hudson Galley — Ship — M-L-007 — S-H-011	Nathaniel Long	Start	Antigua	XXXXXXXXXXXXXX	>	Philadelphia [Pennsylvania]	[18 Dec 1722] / [26 Dec 1722] / [26 Feb 1723]
← M-H-018 / S-H-011 / Page # 45		>	Antigua		[>]	London [England]	
		>	Philadelphia [Pennsylvania]	[29 Nov 1723] / [5 Dec 1723] / [24 Dec 1723]	>	London [England]	
Source: 7:146,148 / 8:22,130,132,138							

Interact 3 — Page 46

Interact	Year / MSTR ID# / SHIP ID#	Ship Name	Type	Burden	First Name	Last Name	Passage Length	Arrival/Departure 1 Port / State/Country	Arrival/Entered Inwards / Custom In/Entered Out / Custom Out/Cleared Out / Departure	Passage Length	Arrival/Departure 2 Port / State/Country	Arrival/Entered Inwards / Custom In/Entered Out / Custom Out/Cleared Out / Departure	Page
3	1723 / M-D-007 / S-E-009	*Esther*	Brigantine		William	Dunlop	Start	Philadelphia [Pennsylvania]	[9 May 1723] XX [27 Jun 1723] XX XXXXXXXXXXXXXX	>	Newfoundland	Never Left For Port / See Next Ship Or Captain	> M-A-009 / S-E-009 / Page # 46
Source: 8:50													
M-D-007 / S-E-009 / Page # 46 <	1723 / M-A-009 / S-E-009	*Esther*	Brigantine		John	Abbot	Start	Philadelphia [Pennsylvania]	XXXXXXXXXXXXXX XX [9 May 1723] XX [27 Jun 1723]	>	Newfoundland		
Source: 8:70													

Interact 4 — Page 46

Interact	Year / MSTR ID# / SHIP ID#	Ship Name	Type	Burden	First Name	Last Name	Passage Length	Arrival/Departure 1 Port / State/Country	Arrival/Entered Inwards / Custom In/Entered Out / Custom Out/Cleared Out / Departure	Passage Length	Arrival/Departure 2 Port / State/Country	Arrival/Entered Inwards / Custom In/Entered Out / Custom Out/Cleared Out / Departure	Page
4	1721 / M-B-029 / S-S-022	*Sarah*	Sloop		James	Bailey	Start	Philadelphia [Pennsylvania]	[24 Aug 1721] [31 Aug 1721]	>	Virginia		> M-J-005 / S-S-022 / Page # 46
							>	Philadelphia [Pennsylvania]	9 Oct 1721 XX [7 Dec 1721] XX XXXXXXXXXXXXXX XXXXXXXXXXXXXX				
Source: 6:94,96,115													
M-B-029 / S-S-022 / Page # 46 <	1721 / M-J-005 / S-S-022	*Sarah*	Sloop		Henry	Johnson	Start	Philadelphia [Pennsylvania]	XX [9 Oct 1721] XX [7 Dec 1721] [7 Dec 1721]	>	North Carolina		
Source: 6:140													

Interact	Ship				Captain / Master		Passage	Arrival / Departure 1		Passage	Arrival / Departure 2		Page
	Year	Name	Type	Burden	First Name	Last Name	Length	Port	Arrival / Entered Inwards / Custom In / Entered Out	Length	Port	Arrival / Entered Inwards / Custom In / Entered Out	
5	MSTR ID# / SHIP ID#	Registry Location						State / Country	Custom Out / Cleared Out / Departure		State / Country	Custom Out / Cleared Out / Departure	47
	Source								Notes				

	1720	*Tryal*	Schooner		Asser	Sharp	Start	Bermuda		>	Philadelphia	13 Aug 1720 [1 Sept 1720]	
	M-S-021										[Pennsylvania]	[15 Sept 1720]	M-D-008 / S-T-006 / Page # 47
	S-T-006						>	Bermuda	XXXXXXXXXXXXX XXXXXXXXXXXXX XXXXXXXXXXXXX				
	5:90,94,99												

M-S-021 < / S-T-006 / Page # 47	1721	*Tryal*	Schooner		Joseph	Dickinson	Start	Bermuda	XXXXXXXXXXXXX	>	Philadelphia	[19 Oct 1721] [23 Nov 1721]	
	M-D-008										[Pennsylvania]	[7 Dec 1721]	
	S-T-006						>	Bermuda					
	6:120,134,140												

Interact	Ship				Captain / Master		Passage	Arrival / Departure 1		Passage	Arrival / Departure 2		Page
	Year	Name	Type	Burden	First Name	Last Name	Length	Port	Arrival / Entered Inwards / Custom In / Entered Out	Length	Port	Arrival / Entered Inwards / Custom In / Entered Out	
6	MSTR ID# / SHIP ID#	Registry Location						State / Country	Custom Out / Cleared Out / Departure		State / Country	Custom Out / Cleared Out / Departure	47
	Source								Notes				

	1721	*Pearl*	Sloop		Samuel	Spofforth	Start	Bermuda		>	Philadelphia	12 Apr 1721 [27 Apr 1721]	
	M-S-022										[Pennsylvania]	[11 May 1721]	
	S-P-016						>	Barbados		>	Philadelphia	7 Aug 1721 [24 Aug 1721]	M-S-023 / S-P-016 / Page # 47
											[Pennsylvania]	[7 Sept 1721]	
							>	Barbados					
	6:38,42,46,90,94,100												

M-S-022 < / S-P-016 / Page # 47	1722	*Pearl*	Sloop		Robert	Spofforth	Start	Bermuda		>	Philadelphia	[19 Apr 1722] [26 Apr 1722]	
	M-S-023										[Pennsylvania]	[17 May 1722]	
	S-P-016						>	Barbados					
	7:46,48,54												

Interact 7 — Page 48

Interact	Year / MSTR ID# / SHIP ID# / Source	Ship Name / Registry Location	Type	Burden	First Name	Last Name	Passage Length	Port / State-Country	Arrival-Entered Inwards / Custom In-Entered Out / Custom Out-Cleared Out / Departure	Passage Length	Port / State-Country	Arrival-Entered Inwards / Custom In-Entered Out / Custom Out-Cleared Out / Departure / Notes	Page
7	1719 – 1720 / M-C-012 / S-R-005	*Rebekah*	Snow		Jehu	Curtis	Start	Philadelphia [Pennsylvania]	[22 Dec 1719]	18 Days	Barbados		48
	Source: 5:2,30,38,41						[>]	Salt Island [Jamaica]		>	Philadelphia [Pennsylvania]	20 Apr 1720 / XXXXXXXXXXXXXXX / XX [7 Jul 1720] XX / XXXXXXXXXXXXXXX → M-S-024 / S-R-005 / Page # 48	

Interact	Year / MSTR ID# / SHIP ID# / Source	Ship Name / Registry Location	Type	Burden	First Name	Last Name	Passage Length	Port / State-Country	Arrival-Entered Inwards / Custom In-Entered Out / Custom Out-Cleared Out / Departure	Passage Length	Port / State-Country	Arrival-Entered Inwards / Custom In-Entered Out / Custom Out-Cleared Out / Departure / Notes	Page
7	← M-C-012 / S-R-005 / Page # 48 — 1720 / M-S-024 / S-R-005	*Rebekah*	Snow		Edward	Sutton	Start	Philadelphia [Pennsylvania]	XX [20 Apr 1720] XX / XXXXXXXXXXXXXX / [7 Jul 1720]	>	Jamaica		48
	Source: 5:72												

Interact 8 — Page 48

Interact	Year / MSTR ID# / SHIP ID# / Source	Ship Name / Registry Location	Type	Burden	First Name	Last Name	Passage Length	Port / State-Country	Arrival-Entered Inwards / Custom In-Entered Out / Custom Out-Cleared Out / Departure	Passage Length	Port / State-Country	Arrival-Entered Inwards / Custom In-Entered Out / Custom Out-Cleared Out / Departure / Notes	Page
8	1720 / M-H-019 / S-T-007	*Three Brothers*	Sloop		John	Hodge	Start	Spanish Town / Jamaica		>	Philadelphia [Pennsylvania]	6 Aug 1720 / [18 Aug 1720] / [25 Aug 1720]	48
	Source: 5:88,90,92						>	Spanish Town / Jamaica	XXXXXXXXXXXXXX / XXXXXXXXXXXXXX / XXXXXXXXXXXXXX			→ M-D-009 / S-T-007 / Page # 48	
8	← M-H-019 / S-T-007 / Page # 48 — 1721 / M-D-009 / S-T-007	*Three Brothers*	Sloop		James	Davis	Start	Spanish Town / Jamaica	XXXXXXXXXXXXXX	>	Philadelphia [Pennsylvania]	8 Jul 1721 / [13 Jul 1721] / [3 Aug 1721]	48
	Source: 6:76,87						>	Spanish Town / Jamaica	XXXXXXXXXXXXXX / XXXXXXXXXXXXXX / XXXXXXXXXXXXXX			→ M-P-012 / S-T-007 / Page # 48	
8	← M-D-009 / S-T-007 / Page # 48 — 1722 / M-P-012 / S-T-007	*Three Brothers*	Sloop		Samuel	Parker	Start	Spanish Town / Jamaica	XXXXXXXXXXXXXX	>	Philadelphia [Pennsylvania]	[16 Aug 1722] / [18 Oct 1722]	48
	Source: 7:96,120						>	Spanish Town / Jamaica					

Interact		Ship				Captain / Master		Passage	Arrival / Departure 1		Passage	Arrival / Departure 2		Page
9	Year	Name	Type	Burden		First Name	Last Name	Length	Port	Arrival / Entered Inwards	Length	Port	Arrival / Entered Inwards	**49**
	MSTR ID#									Custom In / Entered Out			Custom In / Entered Out	
	SHIP ID#	Registry Location							State / Country	Custom Out / Cleared Out		State / Country	Custom Out / Cleared Out	
	Source									Departure		Notes	Departure	

1720	*Three Brothers*	Sloop		William	Davis	Start	Salt Island		>	Barbados			M-S-025
M-D-010							[Jamaica]						S-T-008
S-T-008													Page # 49
						>	Philadelphia	[28 Apr 1720]					
								XX [5 May 1720] XX					
							[Pennsylvania]	XXXXXXXXXXXXXX					
								XXXXXXXXXXXXXX					
5:41													

1720	*Three Brothers*	Sloop		John	Styles	Start	Philadelphia	XX [28 Apr 1720] XX	>	Jamaica			
M-S-025								[5 May 1720]					
S-T-008							[Pennsylvania]	[26 May 1720]					
M-D-010						[>]	Turks Island		>	New York	28 Sept 1720		
S-T-008											[10 Oct 1720]		
Page # 49										[New York]	[24 Oct 1720]		
						>	Antigua						
5:45,56,110,112,120													

Interact		Ship				Captain / Master		Passage	Arrival / Departure 1		Passage	Arrival / Departure 2		Page
10	Year	Name	Type	Burden		First Name	Last Name	Length	Port	Arrival / Entered Inwards	Length	Port	Arrival / Entered Inwards	**49**
	MSTR ID#									Custom In / Entered Out			Custom In / Entered Out	
	SHIP ID#	Registry Location							State / Country	Custom Out / Cleared Out		State / Country	Custom Out / Cleared Out	
	Source									Departure		Notes	Departure	

1720	*Hannah*	Brigantine		Caleb	Jacobs	Start	Philadelphia	[14 Mar 1720]	>	Jamaica	Never Left For Port		M-G-011
M-J-006							[Pennsylvania]	XX [21 Apr 1720] XX			See Next Ship Or Captain		S-H-012
S-H-012								XXXXXXXXXXXXXX					Page # 49
5:27													

1720 – 1721	*Hannah*	Brigantine		Joseph	Griffith	Start	Philadelphia	XXXXXXXXXXXXXX	>	Jamaica			
M-G-011								XX [14 Mar 1720] XX					
S-H-012							[Pennsylvania]	[21 Apr 1720]					
M-J-006						>	Gulf of Florida	Before 6 Apr 1721	&		Ships Crew Saved		
S-H-012								Lost			Ship Lost		
Page # 49						>	Philadelphia	Never Reached Port					
							[Pennsylvania]	Lost					
5:38 / 6:36													

Interact	Year	Ship Name	Type	Burden	Captain / Master First Name	Last Name	Passage Length	Port	Arrival / Entered Inwards / Custom In / Entered Out / Custom Out / Cleared Out / Departure	Passage Length	Port	Arrival / Entered Inwards / Custom In / Entered Out / Custom Out / Cleared Out / Departure	Page
11	MSTR ID# / SHIP ID#	Registry Location						State / Country	Notes		State / Country		**50**
		Source											

Interact 11

	Year	Name	Type	Burden	First Name	Last Name	Length	Port / State-Country	Dates		Port / State-Country	Dates	Link
	1721	*Adventure*	Sloop		James	Ferguson	Start	Boston [Massachusetts]		>	Philadelphia [Pennsylvania]	31 Jul 1721 / XXXXXXXXXXXXXX / XXXXXXXXXXXXXX / XXXXXXXXXXXXXX	
M-F-001 / S-A-003													

XXXXXXXXXX XXXXXXXXXX Captain / Master Changed Ships XXXXXXXXXX XXXXXXXXXX

	Year	Name	Type	Burden	First Name	Last Name	Length	Port / State-Country	Dates		Port / State-Country	Dates	Link
	1721	*Bon-Adventure*	Sloop				Start	Philadelphia [Pennsylvania]	XXXXXXXXXXXXXX / [24 Aug 1721] / [7 Sept 1721] / XXXXXXXXXXXXXX	>	Boston [Massachusetts]	Never Left For Port / See Next Ship Or Captain	M-W-015 / S-B-014 / Page # 50
S-B-014									6:87,94,100				

Link	Year	Name	Type	Burden	First Name	Last Name	Length	Port / State-Country	Dates		Port / State-Country	Dates
M-F-001 / S-B-014 / Page # 50	1721	*Bon-Adventure*	Sloop		Joseph	West	Start	Philadelphia [Pennsylvania]	XXXXXXXXXXXXXX / XX [24 Aug 1721] XX / [14 Sept 1721]	>	Madeira Island [Portugal]	
M-W-015 / S-B-014									6:104			

Interact	Year	Ship Name	Type	Burden	Captain / Master First Name	Last Name	Passage Length	Port	Arrival / Entered Inwards / Custom In / Entered Out / Custom Out / Cleared Out / Departure	Passage Length	Port	Arrival / Entered Inwards / Custom In / Entered Out / Custom Out / Cleared Out / Departure	Page
12	MSTR ID# / SHIP ID#	Registry Location						State / Country	Notes		State / Country		**50**
		Source											

Interact 12

	Year	Name	Type	Burden	First Name	Last Name	Length	Port	Dates		Port	Dates	Link
M-S-026 / S-F-011	1720 – 1721	*Francis & Mary*	Sloop		John	Scott	Start	St Christopher's		>	[Philadelphia] [Pennsylvania]	6 Dec 1720 / [17 Jan 1721] / [2 Mar 1721]	
							>	St Christopher's		>	[Philadelphia] [Pennsylvania]	1 Aug 1721 / [24 Aug 1721] / [21 Sept 1721]	
							>	St Christopher's					

NO SUPPORTING DATA TO LINK TIMELINE

	Year	Name	Type	Burden	First Name	Last Name	Length	Port	Dates		Port	Dates	Link
	1723	*Francis & Mary*	Sloop				Start	St Christopher's		>	Philadelphia [Pennsylvania]	[11 Jul 1723] / XX [29 Aug 1723] XX / XXXXXXXXXXXXXX / XXXXXXXXXXXXXX	M-W-016 / S-F-011 / Page # 50
S-F-011									5:138 / 6:10,23,87,94,106 / 8:76				

Link	Year	Name	Type	Burden	First Name	Last Name	Length	Port	Dates		Port	Dates
M-S-026 / S-F-011 / Page # 50	1723	*Francis & Mary*	Sloop		Garshom	Wilson	Start	Philadelphia [Pennsylvania]	XX [11 Jul 1723] XX / [29 Aug 1723] / [12 Sept 1723]	>	St Christopher's	
M-W-016 / S-F-011									8:94,98			

Interact	Ship				Captain / Master		Passage	Arrival / Departure 1		Passage	Arrival / Departure 2		Page
	Year	Name	Type	Burden	First Name	Last Name	Length	Port	Arrival / Entered Inwards	Length	Port	Arrival / Entered Inwards	
13									Custom In / Entered Out			Custom In / Entered Out	51
	MSTR ID#								Custom Out / Cleared Out			Custom Out / Cleared Out	
	SHIP ID#	Registry Location						State / Country	Departure		State / Country	Departure	
	Source							Notes					

	1719 – 1722	Hanover	Ship		John	Owen	Start	Philadelphia		>			
	M-O-003							[Pennsylvania]	[29 Dec 1719]		South Carolina		
	S-H-013												

| | | | | | | | [>] | | | > | Cowes | | |
| | | | | | | | | Holland | | | [England] | [? Oct 1720] | |

| | | | | | | | > | Bermuda | | > | Delaware River | 6 Apr 1721 | |

M-C-013
S-H-013
Page # 51

							>	Philadelphia	8 Apr 1721	>	Cowes		
									[25 May 1721]				
								[Pennsylvania]	[20 Jul 1721]		[England]		

| | | | | | | | [>] | | | > | Cowes | | |
| | | | | | | | | Holland | | | [England] | | |

							>	Delaware River	3 Oct 1722	>	Philadelphia	[? Oct 1722]	
												XX [5 Feb 1723] XX	
											[Pennsylvania]	XXXXXXXXXXXXXX	
												XXXXXXXXXXXXXX	

XXXXXXXXXX XXXXXXXXXX Captain / Master Changed Ships XXXXXXXXXX XXXXXXXXXX

	1723	Susanna	Sloop				Start	Philadelphia	XXXXXXXXXXXXXX	>	Curacao		
									[4 Apr 1723]				
	S-S-023							[Pennsylvania]	[9 May 1723]				

| 5:4 / 6:6,18,28,36,38,53,79 / 7:114 / 8:34,50 | | | | | | | | (Known Passengers / Palatine) Philadelphia / Inward – 3 Oct 1722 – Count 130+ | | | | | |

	1723	Hanover	Ship		Thomas	Clayton	Start	Philadelphia	XX [? Oct 1722] XX	>	Rotterdam		
									[5 Feb 1723]				
								[Pennsylvania]	[4 Apr 1723]		[Holland]		

M-O-003
S-H-013
Page # 51

<
M-C-013
S-H-013

| 8:12,34 | | | | | | | | | | | | | |

Interact	Ship				Captain / Master		Passage	Arrival / Departure 1		Passage	Arrival / Departure 2		Page
	Year	Name	Type	Burden	First Name	Last Name	Length	Port	Arrival / Entered Inwards	Length	Port	Arrival / Entered Inwards	
14	MSTR ID#								Custom In / Entered Out			Custom In / Entered Out	52
	SHIP ID#	Registry Location						State / Country	Custom Out / Cleared Out		State / Country	Custom Out / Cleared Out	
	Source								Departure		Notes	Departure	

	1719 – 1720	*Three Sisters*	Sloop		Nicholas	Webb	Start	New York	[9 Dec 1719]	>	Barbados	
	M-W-017								(5 Jan 1720)			
	S-T-009							[New York]				
							>	Philadelphia	[28 Apr 1720]	>	Barbados	
								[Pennsylvania]	[19 May 1720]			
							>	Philadelphia	3 Aug 1720	>	Barbados	
									[11 Aug 1720]			
								[Pennsylvania]	[18 Aug 1720]			
							>	Philadelphia	15 Nov 1720	>	Barbados	XXXXXXXXXXXXXX
									[24 Nov 1720]			XXXXXXXXXXXXXX
								[Pennsylvania]	[1 Dec 1720]			XXXXXXXXXXXXXX
	5:2,8,41,53,85,88,90,129,133,136											

> M-B-030
> S-T-009
> Page # 52

	1721	*Three Sisters*	Sloop		James	Brown	Start	Barbados	XXXXXXXXXXXXXX	>	Philadelphia	[27 Apr 1721]
	M-B-030											[4 May 1721]
	S-T-009										[Pennsylvania]	[25 May 1721]
							>	Barbados		>	Philadelphia	8 Aug 1721
												[17 Aug 1721]
											[Pennsylvania]	[31 Aug 1721]
							>	Barbados		>	Philadelphia	13 Nov 1721
											[Pennsylvania]	[30 Nov 1721]
							>	Barbados				
	6:42,44,53,90,92,132,138											

M-W-017
S-T-009
Page # 52

Interact	Ship				Captain / Master		Passage	Arrival / Departure 1		Passage	Arrival / Departure 2		Page
15	Year	Name	Type	Burden	First Name	Last Name	Length	Port	Arrival / Entered Inwards / Custom In / Entered Out	Length	Port	Arrival / Entered Inwards / Custom In / Entered Out	53
	MSTR ID#							State / Country	Custom Out / Cleared Out / Departure		State / Country	Custom Out / Cleared Out / Departure	
	SHIP ID#	Registry Location											
		Source							Notes				

Block 1

	Year	Name	Type		First	Last	Passage	Port	Dates	Passage	Port	Dates	
	1720 – 1721	Martha & Mary	Schooner		Benjamin	Davis	Start	Philadelphia	[16 Jun 1720] [7 Jul 1720]	>	London		
	M-D-011							[Pennsylvania]			[England]	30 Sept 1720	
	S-M-026												
							>	Isle of Wight		>	English Channel	[? Nov 1720]	> M-W-018 / S-M-026 / Page # 53
								[England]	[? Oct 1720]				
							>	Philadelphia	[3 Jan 1721] XX [2 Mar 1721] XX XXXXXXXXXXXXXX XXXXXXXXXXXXXX				
								[Pennsylvania]					
				Source: 5:63,72 / 6:6									

Block 2

M-D-011 / S-M-026 / Page # 53 <	Year	Name	Type	First	Last	Passage	Port	Dates	Passage	Port		M-R-011 / S-M-026 / Page # 53 >
	1721 – 1722	Martha & Mary	Schooner	James	Wilkins	Start	Philadelphia	XX [3 Jan 1721] XX [2 Mar 1721] [16 Mar 1721]	7 Days	Bermuda		
	M-W-018						[Pennsylvania]					
	S-M-026											
						>	Philadelphia	30 Jul 1721 [24 Aug 1721] [14 Sept 1721]	>	Bermuda		
							[Pennsylvania]					
						>	Philadelphia	[23 Nov 1721] [27 Feb 1722] [12 Apr 1722]	>	Bermuda		
							[Pennsylvania]					
						>	Philadelphia	[14 Jun 1722] XX [14 Jun 1722] XX XXXXXXXXXXXXXX XXXXXXXXXXXXXX				
							[Pennsylvania]					
			XXXXXXXXXX XXXXXXXXXX Captain / Master Changed Ships XXXXXXXXXX XXXXXXXXXX									
	1723	St Christopher's	Sloop			Start	Philadelphia	[21 Nov 1723]	>	St Christopher's		
	S-S-024						[Pennsylvania]					
				Source: 6:23,28,87,94,104,134 / 7:23,42,70 / 8:128								

Block 3

M-W-018 / S-M-026 / Page # 53 <	Year	Name	Type	First	Last	Passage	Port	Dates	Passage	Port		
	1722 – 1723	Martha & Mary	Schooner	John	Reeve	Start	Philadelphia	XX [14 Jun 1722] XX [14 Jun 1722] [5 Jul 1722]	>	Bermuda		
	M-R-011						[Pennsylvania]					
	S-M-026											
						>	Philadelphia	[30 Aug 1722] [6 Sept 1722] [13 Sept 1722]	>	North Carolina		
							[Pennsylvania]					
						>	Philadelphia	[25 Apr 1723] [6 Jun 1723] [27 Jun 1723]	>	Antigua		
							[Pennsylvania]					
						>	Philadelphia	[21 Nov 1723] [5 Dec 1723]	>	Antigua		
							[Pennsylvania]					
				Source: 7:70,79,102,106,108 / 8:42,62,70,128,132								

Interact					Captain / Master		Passage		Arrival / Departure 1	Passage		Arrival / Departure 2	Page
	Year	Name	Type	Burden	First Name	Last Name	Length	Port	Arrival / Entered Inwards	Length	Port	Arrival / Entered Inwards	
16	MSTR ID#	Registry Location							Custom In / Entered Out			Custom In / Entered Out	54
	SHIP ID#							State / Country	Custom Out / Cleared Out		State / Country	Custom Out / Cleared Out	
		Source							Departure			Departure	
												Notes	

1720 – 1722	*Sarah*	Sloop		Aaron	Harden / Harding	Start	Philadelphia	[7 Mar 1720] [31 Mar 1720]	>	Barbados		
M-H-020												
S-S-025							[Pennsylvania]					
						>	Philadelphia	22 Jun 1720 [30 Jun 1720] [14 Jul 1720]	>	Antigua		
							[Pennsylvania]					
						>	Philadelphia	7 Nov 1720 [24 Nov 1720] [8 Dec 1720]	>	Barbados		
							[Pennsylvania]					
						[>]	Antigua		>	Anguilla		M-W-019 S-S-025 Page # 54
											8 Feb 1721	
						>	Philadelphia	[16 Mar 1721] [30 Mar 1721] [6 Apr 1721]	>	Barbados		
							[Pennsylvania]					
						>	Philadelphia	7 Jul 1721 [20 Jul 1721] [10 Aug 1721]	>	Milford Haven		
							[Pennsylvania]			[Wales]		
						[>]	Bristol		>	Philadelphia	[31 May 1722] XXXXXXXXXXXXX	
							[England]			[Pennsylvania]	XX [5 Jul 1722] XX XXXXXXXXXXXXX	
	5:24,32,67,70,75,126,133,138 / 6:28,32,34,36,76,79,90 / 7:64											

1722	*Sarah*	Sloop		Mark	Weldon	Start	Philadelphia	XX [31 May 1722] XX XXXXXXXXXXXXX	>	Barbados		
M-H-020 S-S-025 Page # 54	M-W-019 S-S-025						[Pennsylvania]	[5 Jul 1722]				
	7:79											

Interact 17 — Page 55

Interact	Year	Name	Type	Burden	First Name	Last Name	Passage Length	Port	Arrival / Entered Inwards · Custom In / Entered Out · Custom Out / Cleared Out · Departure	Passage Length	Port	Arr/Dep 2	Cross-ref
17	1720	*Britannia*	Snow			Holiman	Start	London [England]		>	Madeira Island [Portugal]		M-R-012 / S-S-B-015 / Page # 55
	M-H-021 / S-B-015						>	Philadelphia [Pennsylvania]	5 Oct 1720 / XX [3 Nov 1720] XX / XXXXXXXXXXXXX / XXXXXXXXXXXXX				

Source: 5:110

Interact	Year	Name	Type	Burden	First Name	Last Name	Passage Length	Port	Arrival / Entered Inwards · Custom In / Entered Out · Custom Out / Cleared Out · Departure	Passage Length	Port	Arr/Dep 2 Departure
17 (M-H-021 / S-B-015 / Page # 55 <)	1720 – 1722	*Britannia*	Snow		John	Read	Start	Philadelphia [Pennsylvania]	XX [5 Oct 1720] XX / [3 Nov 1720] / [8 Dec 1720]	>	London [England]	
	M-R-012 / S-B-015						[>]	Madeira Island [Portugal]		>	London [England]	11 or 12 Jul 1722
							>	Philadelphia [Pennsylvania]	[15 Nov 1722] / [11 Dec 1722] / [18 Dec 1722]	>	Jamaica	

Source: 5:123,138 / 7:112,132,142,146

Interact 18 — Page 55

Interact	Year	Name	Type	Burden	First Name	Last Name	Passage Length	Port	Arrival / Entered Inwards · Custom In / Entered Out · Custom Out / Cleared Out · Departure	Passage Length	Port	Arr/Dep 2 Departure	Cross-ref
18	1720	*Margaret*	Sloop		John	Kirle	Start	Philadelphia [Pennsylvania]	[28 Apr 1720] / [1 Jun 1720]	>	Charles Town / South Carolina	1 Aug 1720	M-C-014 / S-M-027 / Page # 55
	M-K-003 / S-M-027						10 Days	Philadelphia [Pennsylvania]	10 Aug 1720 / [25 Aug 1720] / [6 Oct 1720]	>	South Carolina		

Source: 5:41,58,88,92,110

Interact	Year	Name	Type	Burden	First Name	Last Name	Passage Length	Port	Arrival / Entered Inwards · Custom In / Entered Out · Custom Out / Cleared Out · Departure	Passage Length	Port	Arr/Dep 2
18 (M-K-003 / S-M-027 / Page # 55 <)	1720 – 1721	*Margaret*	Sloop		Robert	Codd	Start	Philadelphia [Pennsylvania]	[27 Dec 1720]	>	South Carolina	
	M-C-014 / S-M-027						>	Philadelphia [Pennsylvania]	[16 Mar 1721] / [20 Apr 1721] / [20 Apr 1721]	>	South Carolina	
							>	Philadelphia [Pennsylvania]	26 Jun 1721			

Source: 6:4,28,40,67

Interact	Ship				Captain / Master		Passage	Arrival / Departure 1		Passage	Arrival / Departure 2		Page
	Year	Name	Type	Burden	First Name	Last Name	Length	Port	Arrival / Entered Inwards / Custom In / Entered Out	Length	Port	Arrival / Entered Inwards / Custom In / Entered Out	
19	MSTR ID#								Custom Out / Cleared Out			Custom Out / Cleared Out	56
	SHIP ID#	Registry Location						State / Country	Departure		State / Country	Departure	
	Source							Notes					

	1720	Arcadia	Sloop		Robert	Gregory	Start			>	Philadelphia	[19 May 1720] / XX [9 Jun 1720] XX	> M-A-010
	M-G-012											XXXXXXXXXXXXXX	S-A-009
	S-A-009										[Pennsylvania]	XXXXXXXXXXXXXX	Page # 56
	5:53												

	1720 – 1722	Arcadia	Sloop		David	Abbot	Start	Philadelphia	XX [19 May 1720] XX / [9 Jun 1720]	>			
	M-A-010								[16 Jun 1720]				
	S-A-009							[Pennsylvania]			South Carolina		
M-G-012							>	Philadelphia	23 Aug 1720 / [1 Sept 1720]	>			
S-A-009									[8 Sept 1720]				
Page # 56								[Pennsylvania]			South Carolina		
							>	Philadelphia	7 Dec 1720 / [20 Dec 1720]	>			
									[27 Dec 1720]				
								[Pennsylvania]			South Carolina		
							>	Philadelphia	[16 Mar 1721] / [23 Mar 1721]	>			
									[30 Mar 1721]				
								[Pennsylvania]			South Carolina		
							>	Philadelphia	31 May 1721 / [8 Jun 1721]	>			
									[15 Jun 1721]				
								[Pennsylvania]			South Carolina		
							>	Philadelphia	9 Aug 1721 / [17 Aug 1721]	>			
									[24 Aug 1721]				
								[Pennsylvania]			South Carolina		
							>	Philadelphia	[9 Nov 1721] / [16 Nov 1721]	>			
									[30 Nov 1721]				
								[Pennsylvania]			South Carolina		
							>	Philadelphia	[22 Mar 1722] / [29 Mar 1722]	>			
									[5 Apr 1722]				
								[Pennsylvania]			South Carolina		
							[>]	Philadelphia	[9 Aug 1722]	>			
								[Pennsylvania]			South Carolina		
	5:60,63,92,94,96,138 / 6:2,4,28,32,34,56,58,60,90,92,94,130,132,138 / 7:32,34,38,40,94												

Interact	Ship				Captain / Master		Passage	Arrival / Departure 1		Passage	Arrival / Departure 2		Page
	Year	Name	Type	Burden	First Name	Last Name	Length	Port	Arrival / Entered Inwards / Custom In / Entered Out	Length	Port	Arrival / Entered Inwards / Custom In / Entered Out	
20	MSTR ID#	Registry Location						State / Country	Custom Out / Cleared Out / Departure		State / Country	Custom Out / Cleared Out / Departure	57
	SHIP ID#												
	Source							Notes					

1722	*Sarah & Mary*	Sloop		William	Beeke	Start			>	Philadelphia	[5 Apr 1722] / [26 Apr 1722]
M-B-031							North Carolina			[Pennsylvania]	[7 Jun 1722]
S-S-026											

> M-M-011 / S-S-026 / Page # 57

	>	Barbados		>	Philadelphia	[6 Sept 1722]
					XX [15 Nov 1722] XX
				[Pennsylvania]	XXXXXXXXXXXXXX / XXXXXXXXXXXXXX

XXXXXXXXXX XXXXXXXXXX Captain / Master Relieved And Then Retook Command XXXXXXXXXX XXXXXXXXXX

M-M-011 / S-S-026 / Page # 57 <

1723 – 1724	*Sarah & Mary*	Sloop				Start	Philadelphia	XX [18 Apr 1723] XX / [25 Apr 1723]	>	Barbados
							[Pennsylvania]	[21 May 1723]		
S-S-026										
						>	Philadelphia	[6 Sept 1723] / [26 Sept 1723]	>	Barbados
							[Pennsylvania]	[11 Oct 1723]		
						[>]	Philadelphia		>	Barbados
							[Pennsylvania]	[16 Jul 1724]		

7:40,48,68,106 / 8:42,58,96,103,109 / 22:239

1722 – 1723	*Sarah & Mary*	Sloop		Isaac	Morris	Start	Philadelphia	XX [6 Sept 1722] XX / [15 Nov 1722]	>	Barbados
M-M-011							[Pennsylvania]	[11 Dec 1722]		
S-S-026										

MB-031 / S-S-026 / Page # 57 <

> M-B-031 / S-S-026 / Page # 57

	>	Philadelphia	[18 Apr 1723] / XX [25 Apr 1723] XX
		[Pennsylvania]	XXXXXXXXXXXXXX / XXXXXXXXXXXXXX

7:132,142 / 8:40

Interact	Ship				Captain / Master		Passage	Arrival / Departure 1		Passage	Arrival / Departure 2		Page
	Year	Name	Type	Burden	First Name	Last Name	Length	Port	Arrival / Entered Inwards	Length	Port	Arrival / Entered Inwards	
21	MSTR ID#								Custom In / Entered Out			Custom In / Entered Out	58
	SHIP ID#	Registry Location						State / Country	Custom Out / Cleared Out		State / Country	Custom Out / Cleared Out	
									Departure			Departure	
	Source							Notes					

	1720	Beginning	Sloop		Joseph	Royal	Start	New York	[6 Jun 1720]	>		[? ? 1720]	M-G-013
	M-R-013											XX [10 Nov 1720] XX	S-B-016
	S-B-016							[New York]	[6 Jun 1720]		Pennsylvania	XXXXXXXXXXXXXX	Page # 58
		5:60										XXXXXXXXXXXXXX	

	1720	Sea Flower	Sloop		William	Goddard	Start	Lewes		>	Philadelphia	[23 Feb 1720]	
	M-G-013											[7 Mar 1720]	
	S-S-027							Delaware			[Pennsylvania]	[7 Mar 1720]	
							>	Bermuda		>	Philadelphia	[19 May 1720]	
												XXXXXXXXXXXXXX	
											[Pennsylvania]	XXXXXXXXXXXXXX	
												XXXXXXXXXXXXXX	

XXXXXXXXXX XXXXXXXXXX Captain / Master Changed Ships XXXXXXXXXX XXXXXXXXXX

	1720 – 1721	Beginning	Sloop				Start	Philadelphia	XX [? ? 1720] XX	>	Bermuda		
									[10 Nov 1720]				
	S-B-016							[Pennsylvania]	[24 Nov 1720]				
M-R-013							[>]	Anguilla	[20 Apr 1721]	>	Philadelphia	[27 Jul 1721]	M-F-007
S-B-016												XX [3 Aug 1721] XX	S-B-016
Page # 58											[Pennsylvania]	XXXXXXXXXXXXXX	Page # 58
							>	Barbados	Never Left For Port				
									See Next Ship Or Captain				

XXXXXXXXXX XXXXXXXXXX Captain / Master Relieved And Then Retook Command XXXXXXXXXX XXXXXXXXXX

	1722	Beginning	Sloop				Start	Philadelphia	XX [? ? 1721] XX	>	South Carolina		
									[15 Mar 1722]				
	S-B-016							[Pennsylvania]	[12 Apr 1722]				
M-F-007							>	Philadelphia	[30 Aug 1722]	[>]	North Carolina		
S-B-016								[Pennsylvania]					
Page # 58							>	Philadelphia	[15 Nov 1722]				
								[Pennsylvania]					
		5:20,24,53,126,133 / 6:40,84 / 7:32,42,102,132											

	1721	Beginning	Sloop		Thomas	Flemming	Start	Philadelphia	XXXXXXXXXXXXXX	>	Barbados		M-G-013
	M-F-007								XX [27 Jul 1721] XX				S-B-016
M-G-013	S-B-016							[Pennsylvania]	[3 Aug 1721]				Page # 58
S-B-016							[>]	Philadelphia	[? ? 1721]				
Page # 58									XX [15 Mar 1722] XX				
								[Pennsylvania]	XXXXXXXXXXXXXX				
		6:87							XXXXXXXXXXXXXX				

Interact	Ship				Captain / Master		Passage	Arrival / Departure 1		Passage	Arrival / Departure 2		Page
22	Year	Name	Type	Burden	First Name	Last Name	Length	Port / State / Country	Arrival / Entered Inwards / Custom In / Entered Out / Custom Out / Cleared Out / Departure	Length	Port / State / Country	Arrival / Entered Inwards / Custom In / Entered Out / Custom Out / Cleared Out / Departure	**59**
	MSTR ID#	Registry Location										Notes	
	SHIP ID#	Source											

Row group 1

1723	Bristol	Brigantine		Thomas	Little	Start	Philadelphia [Pennsylvania]	[9 May 1723] / XX [6 Jun 1723] XX / XXXXXXXXXXXXXX	>	Jamaica	Never Left For Port / See Next Ship Or Captain
M-L-008											
S-B-017											

> M-P-013 / S-B-017 / Page # 59

XXXXXXXXXX XXXXXXXXXX Captain / Master Changed Ships XXXXXXXXXX XXXXXXXXXX

1723	Neptune	Brigantine				Start	Philadelphia [Pennsylvania]	XXXXXXXXXXXXXX / [30 May 1723] / [6 Jun 1723]	>	Antigua	
S-N-009											
						>	St John's / Antigua	20 Sept 1723 / Lost	>	St John's / Antigua	Lost In Harbor / Hurricane

Source: 8:50,60,62,126

Row group 2

1720	Sarah	Brigantine		Joseph	Prichard	Start	Philadelphia [Pennsylvania]	[7 Mar 1720] / [31 Mar 1720]	>	South Carolina	
M-P-013											
S-S-028											
						[>]	Holland		>	Plymouth [England]	
						9 Weeks	Philadelphia [Pennsylvania]	6 Dec 1720 / XXXXXXXXXXXXXX / XXXXXXXXXXXXXX / XXXXXXXXXXXXXX			

XXXXXXXXXX XXXXXXXXXX Captain / Master Changed Ships XXXXXXXXXX XXXXXXXXXX

1721 – 1722	Sarah	Snow				Start	Philadelphia [Pennsylvania]	XXXXXXXXXXXXXX / [17 Jan 1721] / [17 Jan 1721]	>	Maryland	
S-S-029											
						[>]	Holland		>	Plymouth [England]	
						>	Philadelphia [Pennsylvania]	[9 Nov 1721] / [23 Nov 1721] / [7 Dec 1721]	>	Jamaica	

> M-L-009 / S-S-029 / Page # 60

| | | | | | | [>] | Holland | | > | Plymouth [England] | |
| | | | | | | > | Philadelphia [Pennsylvania] | [18 Oct 1722] / XXXXXXXXXXXXXX / XX [2 May 1723] XX / XXXXXXXXXXXXXX | | | |

XXXXXXXXXX XXXXXXXXXX Captain / Master Changed Ships XXXXXXXXXX XXXXXXXXXX

1723	Bristol	Brigantine				Start	Philadelphia [Pennsylvania]	XXXXXXXXXXXXXX / XX [9 May 1723] XX / [6 Jun 1723]	>	Jamaica	
S-B-017											
						>	Philadelphia [Pennsylvania]	[4 Oct 1723] / [24 Oct 1723]	>	Bristol [England]	

M-L-008 / S-B-017 / Page # 59 <

Source: 5:24,32,141 / 6:10,130,134,140 / 7:120 / 8:62,106,109,114

Interact	Ship				Captain / Master		Passage	Arrival / Departure 1		Passage	Arrival / Departure 2		Page
	Year	Name	Type	Burden	First Name	Last Name	Length	Port	Arrival / Entered Inwards	Length	Port	Arrival / Entered Inwards	
22									Custom In / Entered Out			Custom In / Entered Out	60
	MSTR ID#							State / Country	Custom Out / Cleared Out		State / Country	Custom Out / Cleared Out	
	SHIP ID#	Registry Location							Departure			Departure	
	Source							Notes					

M-P-013	1723	Sarah	Snow		Lawrence	Lawrence	Start	Philadelphia	XX [18 Oct 1722] XX	>	Jamaica		M-P-014
S-S-029	M-L-009								XXXXXXXXXXXXXX				S-S-029
Page # 59	S-S-029							[Pennsylvania]	[2 May 1723]				Page # 60
							>	Philadelphia	[15 Aug 1723]	>	Jamaica	Never Left For Port	
									[22 Aug 1723]				
								[Pennsylvania]	XX[26 Sept 1723] XX			See Next Ship Or Captain	
									XXXXXXXXXXXXXX				
	8:46,88,91												

M-L-009	1723	Sarah	Snow		Laborious	Pearce	Start	Philadelphia	XXXXXXXXXXXXXX	>	Jamaica		
S-S-029	M-P-014								XX [22 Aug 1723] XX				
Page # 60	S-S-029							[Pennsylvania]	[26 Sept 1723]				
	8:103												

Interact		Ship				Captain / Master		Passage	Arrival / Departure 1		Passage	Arrival / Departure 2		Page
	Year	Name	Type	Burden		First Name	Last Name	Length	Port	Arrival / Entered Inwards / Custom In / Entered Out / Custom Out / Cleared Out / Departure	Length	Port	Arrival / Entered Inwards / Custom In / Entered Out / Custom Out / Cleared Out / Departure	
23	MSTR ID# / SHIP ID#	Registry Location							State / Country			State / Country		61
	Source								Notes					

Row 1

23										
	1720	Dove	Brigantine		Thomas	Montague	Start	Philadelphia	>	Barbados
	M-M-012							[Pennsylvania]	[14 Jul 1720]	
	S-D-010									
	5:75									

Cross-ref: > M-C-015 / S-D-010 / Page # 61

Row 2

M-M-012 / S-D-010 / Page # 61 <	1721	Dove	Brigantine		John	Crate	Start	London [England]	>	Isle of May [Scotland]
	M-C-015									
	S-D-010					>	Philadelphia [Pennsylvania]	26 Apr 1721 / XX [18 May 1721] XX / XXXXXXXXXXXXX / XXXXXXXXXXXXX		

6:42,44

Notes: Captain Died – John Crate / Crane - Late Mate Now Master

Cross-ref: > M-S-027 / S-D-010 / Page # 61

Row 3

	1719 – 1720	Mary Galley	Ship		Stephen	Simmons	Start	London [England]	>	Philadelphia [Pennsylvania]	[22 Dec 1719] / [2 Feb 1720] / [31 Mar 1720]
	M-S-027										
	S-M-028						>	Barbados			

XXXXXXXXX XXXXXXXXXX Captain / Master Changed Ships XXXXXXXXX XXXXXXXXXX

M-C-015 / S-D-010 / Page # 61 <	1721 – 1722	Dove	Brigantine				Start	Philadelphia [Pennsylvania]	XX 26 Apr 1721 XX / [18 May 1721] / [13 Jul 1721]	>	London [England]
	S-D-010						>	Prime Hook [Delaware]	[9 Jan 1722] / To Avoid the Driving Ice	>	Philadelphia [Pennsylvania]	[6 Feb 1722] / XX [21 Mar 1722] XX / XXXXXXXXXXXXX / XXXXXXXXXXXXX

Cross-ref: > M-A-011 / S-D-010 / Page # 61

XXXXXXXXX XXXXXXXXXX Captain / Master Changed Ships XXXXXXXXX XXXXXXXXXX

	1722	Sarah & Mary	Sloop				Start	Philadelphia [Pennsylvania]	XXXXXXXXXXXXX / [8 Nov 1722] / [11 Dec 1722]	>	Madeira Island [Portugal]
	S-S-030										

5:2,14,32 / 6:49,71,76 / 7:4,13,126,130,142

Row 4

M-S-027 / S-D-010 / Page # 61 <	1722	Dove	Brigantine		Lawrence	Anderson	Start	Philadelphia [Pennsylvania]	XX [6 Feb 1722] XX / [21 Mar 1722] / [12 Apr 1722]	>	New England
	M-A-011										
	S-D-010										
	7:34,42										

Cross-ref: > M-N-004 / S-D-010 / Page # 62

Interact	Ship				Captain / Master		Passage	Arrival / Departure 1		Passage	Arrival / Departure 2		Page
	Year	Name	Type	Burden	First Name	Last Name	Length	Port	Arrival / Entered Inwards	Length	Port	Arrival / Entered Inwards	
23	MSTR ID#								Custom In / Entered Out			Custom In / Entered Out	**62**
	SHIP ID#	Registry Location						State / Country	Custom Out / Cleared Out		State / Country	Custom Out / Cleared Out	
									Departure			Departure	
	Source									Notes			

	1722 – 1724	*Dove*	Brigantine		Henry	Norwood	Start	Madeira Island		>	London		
	M-N-004												
	S-D-010							[Portugal]			[England]		
M-A-011 <							>	Philadelphia	[18 Dec 1722]	[>]	Barbados		
S-D-010									[5 Feb 1723]				
Page # 61								[Pennsylvania]					
							>	Philadelphia	[18 Jul 1723]	>	Barbados		
									[25 Jul 1723]				
								[Pennsylvania]	[15 Aug 1723]				
							>	Philadelphia	[25 Jun 1724]	>	Jamaica		
								[Pennsylvania]	[16 Jul 1724]				
	7:146 / 8:12,78,81,88 / 22:236,239												

Interact		Ship				Captain / Master		Passage	Arrival / Departure 1		Passage	Arrival / Departure 2		Page
	Year	Name	Type	Burden		First Name	Last Name	Length	Port	Arrival / Entered Inwards / Custom In / Entered Out	Length	Port	Arrival / Entered Inwards / Custom In / Entered Out	
24	MSTR ID#									Custom Out / Cleared Out / Departure			Custom Out / Cleared Out / Departure	63
	SHIP ID#	Registry Location							State / Country			State / Country		
		Source								Notes				

	1720	*Dolphin*	Sloop			John	Richmond	Start	Barbados		>	Philadelphia	[5 May 1720] [1 Jun 1720]	
	M-R-014											[Pennsylvania]	XX [14 Jul 1720] XX XXXXXXXXXXXXXX	
	S-D-011													> M-T-010 / S-D-011 / Page # 64
								>	Barbados	Never Left For Port / See Next Ship Or Captain				

XXXXXXXXXX XXXXXXXXXX Captain / Master Changed Ships XXXXXXXXXX XXXXXXXXXX

	1720 – 1722	*Betty*	Ship					Start	Philadelphia	XXXXXXXXXXXXXX [24 Nov 1720] [27 Dec 1720]	>	Jamaica		
	S-B-018								[Pennsylvania]					
								[>]	London		>	Philadelphia	[6 Feb 1722]	
									[England]			[Pennsylvania]	[12 Apr 1722]	
								>	Newfoundland		[>]	London		
												[England]		
								>	Philadelphia	[23 Nov 1722] [11 Dec 1722] [18 Dec 1722]	>	Madeira Island		
									[Pennsylvania]			[Portugal]		

XXXXXXXXXX XXXXXXXXXX Captain / Master Changed Ships XXXXXXXXXX XXXXXXXXXX

	1723	*Richmond*	Ship					Start	Philadelphia	[24 Oct 1723] [17 Dec 1723]	>	London		
	S-R-006								[Pennsylvania]			[England]		
		5:45,58,133 / 6:4 / 7:13,42,136,142,146 / 8:106,110,114							Advertising that he will be headed to London Soon. (4 Oct – 11 Oct 1723)					

Interact	Ship				Captain / Master		Passage	Arrival / Departure 1		Passage	Arrival / Departure 2		Page
	Year	Name	Type	Burden	First Name	Last Name	Length	Port	Arrival / Entered Inwards	Length	Port	Arrival / Entered Inwards	
24									Custom In / Entered Out			Custom In / Entered Out	64
	MSTR ID#								Custom Out / Cleared Out			Custom Out / Cleared Out	
	SHIP ID#	Registry Location						State / Country	Departure		State / Country	Departure	
		Source							Notes				

	1720 – 1723	*Dolphin*	Sloop		Henry	Taylor	Start	Philadelphia	XXXXXXXXXXXXXX XX [1 Jun 1720] XX [14 Jul 1720]	>	Barbados		
	M-T-010												
	S-D-011							[Pennsylvania]					
							>	Philadelphia	7 Nov 1720 [17 Nov 1720] [8 Dec 1720]	>	Barbados		
								[Pennsylvania]					
							>	Salt Island		>	Philadelphia	[20 Apr 1721] [11 May 1721] [1 Jun 1721]	
								[Jamaica]			[Pennsylvania]		
							>	Barbados		>	Philadelphia	[7 Sept 1721] [9 Nov 1721] [7 Dec 1721]	
											[Pennsylvania]		
M-R-014							>	Barbados		>	Anguilla		
S-D-011													
Page # 63							>	Delaware River	22 Mar 1722	>	Philadelphia	[29 Mar 1722] [12 Apr 1722]	
											[Pennsylvania]		
							>	Jamaica		>	Philadelphia	[6 Sept 1722] [23 Nov 1722] [18 Dec 1722]	
											[Pennsylvania]		
							>	Barbados		>	Philadelphia	[25 Apr 1723] [2 May 1723] [30 May 1723]	
											[Pennsylvania]		
							>	Barbados		>	Philadelphia	[24 Oct 1723] [31 Oct 1723] [21 Nov 1723]	
											[Pennsylvania]		
							>	Barbados					
	5:75,126,129,138 / 6:40,46,56,100,130,140 / 7:34,38,42,106,136,146 / 8:42,46,60,114,118,128												

Interact	Year	Name	Type	Burden	First Name	Last Name	Passage Length	A/D 1 Port	A/D 1 State/Country	A/D 1 Dates	Passage Length	A/D 2 Port	A/D 2 State/Country	A/D 2 Dates	Page
										Arrival / Entered Inwards — Custom In / Entered Out — Custom Out / Cleared Out — Departure					
25	MSTR ID# / SHIP ID# — Registry Location				Captain / Master										**65**

Source

Interact	Year / ID	Ship Name	Type	First / Last	Pass.	A/D 1 Port / State	A/D 1 Dates	Pass.	A/D 2 Port / State	A/D 2 Dates	Link
25	1720 / M-G-014 / S-E-010	*Endeavor*	Sloop	Alexander Gordon	Start	Annapolis [Maryland]		>	Philadelphia [Pennsylvania]	25 Jul 1720 / XX [11 Aug 1720] XX / XXXXXXXXXXXXX / XXXXXXXXXXXXX	> M-T-011 / S-E-010 / Page # 65

XXXXXXXXXX XXXXXXXXXX Captain / Master Changed Ships XXXXXXXXXX XXXXXXXXXX

| | 1720 / S-H-014 | *Hastings* | Sloop | | Start | Philadelphia [Pennsylvania] | XXXXXXXXXXXXX / [10 Nov 1720] / XX [17 Nov 1720] XX / XXXXXXXXXXXXX | > | Patuxent [Maryland] | Never Left For Port / See Next Ship Or Captain | > M-R-015 / S-H-014 / Page # 67 |

XXXXXXXXXX XXXXXXXXXX Captain / Master Changed Ships XXXXXXXXXX XXXXXXXXXX

	1721 / S-R-007	*Robert & James*	Sloop		Start	Maryland		>	Philadelphia [Pennsylvania]	[20 Apr 1721] / [25 May 1721] / [1 Jun 1721]	
					>	Curacao		[>]	Jamaica		> M-R-016 / S-R-007 / Page # 67
					>	Philadelphia [Pennsylvania]	[19 Oct 1721] / XX [24 May 1722] XX / XXXXXXXXXXXXX / XXXXXXXXXXXXX				

Source: 5:82,126 / 6:40,53,56,120

Interact	Year / ID	Ship Name	Type	First / Last	Pass.	A/D 1 Port / State	A/D 1 Dates	Pass.	A/D 2 Port / State	A/D 2 Dates	Link
25	1720 / M-T-011 / S-?-016		Sloop	Thomas Terrell	Start	Providence		>	Philadelphia [Pennsylvania]	19 Jul 1720 / XXXXXXXXXXXXX / XXXXXXXXXXXXX / XXXXXXXXXXXXX	

XXXXXXXXXX XXXXXXXXXX Captain / Master Changed Ships XXXXXXXXXX XXXXXXXXXX

| M-G-014 / S-E-010 / Page # 65 < | 1720 / S-E-010 | *Endeavor* | Sloop | | Start | Philadelphia [Pennsylvania] | XX 25 Jul 1720 XX / [11 Aug 1720] / XX [18 Aug 1720] XX / XXXXXXXXXXXXX | > | Providence | Never Left For Port / See Next Ship Or Captain | > M-S-028 / S-E-010 / Page # 65 |

XXXXXXXXXX XXXXXXXXXX Captain / Master Relieved And Then Retook Command XXXXXXXXXX XXXXXXXXXX

| M-S-028 / S-E-010 / Page # 65 < | 1720 / S-E-010 | *Endeavor* | Sloop | | Start | Philadelphia [Pennsylvania] | XX 17 Oct 1720 XX / [27 Oct 1720] / [10 Nov 1720] | > | New Providence | XXXXXXXXXXXXX / XXXXXXXXXXXXX / XXXXXXXXXXXXX | > M-P-015 / S-E-010 / Page # 65 |

Source: 5:78,88,120,126

Interact	Year / ID	Ship Name	Type	First / Last	Pass.	A/D 1 Port / State	A/D 1 Dates	Pass.	A/D 2 Port / State	A/D 2 Dates	Link
25 / M-T-011 / S-E-010 / Page # 65 <	1720 / M-S-028 / S-E-010	*Endeavor*	Sloop	John Searle	Start	Philadelphia [Pennsylvania]	XXXXXXXXXXXXX / XX [11 Aug 1720] XX / [18 Aug 1720]	>	Providence		> M-T-011 / S-E-010 / Page # 65
					>	Philadelphia [Pennsylvania]	17 Oct 1720 / XX [27 Oct 1720] XX / XXXXXXXXXXXXX / XXXXXXXXXXXXX				

Source: 5:90,115

Interact	Year / ID	Ship Name	Type	First / Last	Pass.	A/D 1 Port / State	A/D 1 Dates	Pass.	A/D 2 Port / State	A/D 2 Dates	Link
25 / M-T-011 / S-E-010 / Page # 65 <	1721 / M-P-015 / S-E-010	*Endeavor*	Sloop	Thomas Petty	Start	New Providence	XXXXXXXXXXXXX	>	Philadelphia [Pennsylvania]	1 Aug 1721 / [17 Aug 1721] / [24 Aug 1721]	> M-B-032 / S-E-010 / Page # 66
					>	New Providence					

Source: 6:87,92,94

Interact														Page
	Ship				Captain / Master		Passage	Arrival / Departure 1		Passage	Arrival / Departure 2			
25	Year	Name	Type	Burden	First Name	Last Name	Length	Port	Arrival / Entered Inwards / Custom In / Entered Out	Length	Port	Arrival / Entered Inwards / Custom In / Entered Out		66
	MSTR ID#								Custom Out / Cleared Out			Custom Out / Cleared Out		
	SHIP ID#	Registry Location						State / Country	Departure		State / Country	Departure		
	Source							Notes						

M-P-015 / S-E-010 / Page # 65

Interact	Year	Name	Type	First Name	Last Name	Passage	Port 1	Dates 1	Passage	Port 2	Dates 2
	1722 / M-B-032 / S-E-010	Endeavor	Sloop	John	Bennett	Start	New Providence		>	Philadelphia [Pennsylvania]	[3 Oct 1722] / [18 Oct 1722] / [8 Nov 1722]
						>	New Providence				

XXXXXXXXX XXXXXXXXX Captain / Master Changed Ships XXXXXXXXX XXXXXXXXX

| | 1723 / S-J-012 | Joseph | Ship | | | Start | New Castle [Delaware] | | > | Philadelphia [Pennsylvania] | [31 Oct 1723] / [31 Oct 1723] / [17 Dec 1723] |
| | | | | | | > | Liverpool [England] | | | | |

Source: 7:114,120,130 / 8:118,136

M-R-016 / S-A-008 / Page # 67

Interact	Year	Name	Type	First Name	Last Name	Passage	Port 1	Dates 1	Passage	Port 2	Dates 2
	1720 – 1721 / M-P-016 / S-B-008	Betty	Sloop	Anthony	Peel	Start	Philadelphia [Pennsylvania]	[22 Dec 1719]	>	Barbados	Before 24 Mar 1720
						[>]	Salt Island [Jamaica]		>	Philadelphia [Pennsylvania]	20 Apr 1720 / [16 Jun 1720] / [21 Jul 1720]
						>	Suriname		>	Philadelphia [Pennsylvania]	[13 Dec 1720] / [20 Apr 1721] / [1 Jun 1721]
						>	Suriname		>	Philadelphia [Pennsylvania]	[9 Nov 1721] / XX [12 Apr 1722] XX / XXXXXXXXXXXXXX XXXXXXXXXXXXXX

(→ M-G-003 / S-B-008 / Page # 68)

XXXXXXXXX XXXXXXXXX Captain / Master Changed Ships XXXXXXXXX XXXXXXXXX

| | 1722 / S-A-008 | Anne | Sloop | | | Start | Philadelphia [Pennsylvania] | XX [5 Apr 1722] XX / [19 Apr 1722] / [26 Apr 1722] | > | Virginia | |
| | | | | | | > | Philadelphia [Pennsylvania] | [19 Jul 1722] / XX [9 Aug 1722] XX / XXXXXXXXXXXXXX XXXXXXXXXXXXXX | | | |

(→ M-G-001 / S-A-008 / Page # 68)

XXXXXXXXX XXXXXXXXX Captain / Master Changed Ships XXXXXXXXX XXXXXXXXX

	1723 / S-W-010	Whitehaven	Sloop			Start	Philadelphia [Pennsylvania]	[2 May 1723] / [16 May 1723]	>	Antigua	
						>	Philadelphia [Pennsylvania]	[19 Sept 1723] / [4 Oct 1723] / [17 Oct 1723]	>	Boston [Massachusetts]	
						>	Philadelphia [Pennsylvania]	[21 Nov 1723] / [29 Nov 1723] / [24 Dec 1723]	>	Antigua	

Source: 5:2,30,38,63,78,141 / 6:40,56,130 / 7:46,48,85 / 8:46,54,100,106,112,128,130,138

Interact	Ship				Captain / Master		Passage	Arrival / Departure 1		Passage	Arrival / Departure 2		Page
	Year	Name	Type	Burden	First Name	Last Name	Length	Port	Arrival / Entered Inwards / Custom In / Entered Out / Custom Out / Cleared Out / Departure	Length	Port	Arrival / Entered Inwards / Custom In / Entered Out / Custom Out / Cleared Out / Departure	
25	MSTR ID#							State / Country			State / Country		**67**
	SHIP ID#	Registry Location										Notes	
	Source												

Interact	Year / MSTR ID# / SHIP ID#	Name	Type	Captain First	Captain Last	Length	Port / State-Country	Dates	Length	Port / State-Country	Dates	Page
	1719 – 1721 / M-R-016 / S-S-031	*Sarah*	Sloop	Shadlock	Rivers	Start	Antigua		>	Philadelphia [Pennsylvania]	[22 Dec 1719] [7 Mar 1720] [31 Mar 1720]	
						>	St Christopher's		>	Philadelphia [Pennsylvania]	19 Jul 1720 [4 Aug 1720] [25 Aug 1720]	
						>	Jamaica		>	Philadelphia [Pennsylvania]	6 Dec 1720 [31 Jan 1721] [2 Mar 1721]	
						>	Antigua		>	Philadelphia [Pennsylvania]	[15 Jun 1721] [6 Jul 1721] [13 Jul 1721]	
						>	Jamaica		>	Philadelphia [Pennsylvania]	[19 Oct 1721] [23 Nov 1721] [7 Dec 1721]	
						>	Jamaica	XXXXXXXXXXXXXX XXXXXXXXXXXXXX XXXXXXXXXXXXXX				

XXXXXXXXXX XXXXXXXXXX Captain / Master Changed Ships XXXXXXXXXX XXXXXXXXXX

Interact	Year / MSTR ID# / SHIP ID#	Name	Type	Captain First	Captain Last	Length	Port / State-Country	Dates	Length	Port / State-Country	Dates	Page
	1722 / S-A-008	*Anne*	Sloop			Start	Jamaica	XXXXXXXXXXXXXX	>	Philadelphia [Pennsylvania]	[5 Apr 1722] XX [19 Apr 1722] XX XXXXXXXXXXXXXX XXXXXXXXXXXXXX	> M-P-016 / S-A-008 / Page # 66

XXXXXXXXXX XXXXXXXXXX Captain / Master Changed Ships XXXXXXXXXX XXXXXXXXXX

Interact	Year / MSTR ID# / SHIP ID#	Name	Type	Captain First	Captain Last	Length	Port / State-Country	Dates	Length	Port / State-Country	Dates	Page
M-G-014 / S-R-007 / Page # 65 <	1722 – 1723 / S-R-007	*Robert & James*	Sloop			Start	Philadelphia [Pennsylvania]	XX [19 Oct 1721] XX [24 May 1722] [14 Jun 1722]	>	St Christopher's		
						>	Philadelphia [Pennsylvania]	[27 Sept 1722] [23 Nov 1722] [11 Dec 1722]	>	St Christopher's		> M-B-033 / S-R-007 / Page # 67
						>	Philadelphia [Pennsylvania]	[25 Apr 1723] [2 May 1723] XX [16 May 1723] XX XXXXXXXXXXXXXX	>	South Carolina	Never Left For Port See Next Ship Or Captain	

5:2,24,32,78,86,92,138 / 6:14,23,60,71,76,120,134,140 / 7:40,60,70,112,136,142 / 8:42,46

Interact	Year / MSTR ID# / SHIP ID#	Name	Type	Captain First	Captain Last	Length	Port / State-Country	Dates	Length	Port / State-Country	Dates
M-R-016 / S-R-007 / Page # 67 <	1723 / M-B-033 / S-R-007	*Robert & James*	Sloop	Robert	Bird	Start	Philadelphia [Pennsylvania]	XXXXXXXXXXXXXX XX [2 May 1723] XX [16 May 1723]	>	South Carolina	Before 29 Jul 1723
						>	29 Jul 1723 – Lost Mast / Drove on Shore 20 Miles to the Southward of Sene Puxon		&	Ships Crew & Cargo Saved Ship Lost & Cargo Was Damaged	

8:54,91

Interact	Year / MSTR ID# / SHIP ID#	Name	Type	Captain First	Captain Last	Length	Port / State-Country	Dates	Length	Port / State-Country	Dates
M-G-014 / S-H-014 / Page # 65 <	1720 / M-R-015 / S-H-014	*Hastings*	Sloop	John	Rice	Start	Philadelphia [Pennsylvania]	XXXXXXXXXXXXXX XX [10 Nov 1720] XX [17 Nov 1720]	>	Patuxent [Maryland]	

5:129

Interact		Ship				Captain / Master		Passage	Arrival / Departure 1		Passage	Arrival / Departure 2		Page
	Year	Name	Type	Burden		First Name	Last Name	Length	Port	Arrival / Entered Inwards	Length	Port	Arrival / Entered Inwards	
25	MSTR ID#									Custom In / Entered Out			Custom In / Entered Out	68
	SHIP ID#	Registry Location							State / Country	Custom Out / Cleared Out		State / Country	Custom Out / Cleared Out	
		Source								Departure		Notes	Departure	

M-P-016	1722	*Betty*	Sloop			Joseph	Griffins	Start	Philadelphia	XX [9 Nov 1721] XX	>	Jamaica	
S-B-008 <	M-G-003									[12 Apr 1722]			
	S-B-008								[Pennsylvania]	[17 May 1722]			
Page # 66		7:42,58											

M-P-016	1722	*Anne*	Sloop			Neil	Gray	Start	Philadelphia	XX [19 Jul 1722] XX	>	Barbados	
S-A-008 <	M-G-001									[9 Aug 1722]			
	S-A-008								[Pennsylvania]	[23 Aug 1722]			
Page # 66		7:94,99											

Interact	Ship				Captain / Master		Passage	Arrival / Departure 1		Passage	Arrival / Departure 2		Page
	Year	Name	Type	Burden	First Name	Last Name	Length	Port	Arrival / Entered Inwards / Custom In / Entered Out	Length	Port	Arrival / Entered Inwards / Custom In / Entered Out	
26	MSTR ID#							State / Country	Custom Out / Cleared Out / Departure		State / Country	Custom Out / Cleared Out / Departure	69
	SHIP ID#	Registry Location											
	Source							Notes					

	1719				Reeves	Holt	Start	Philadelphia	XXXXXXXXXXXXXX XXXXXXXXXXXXXX XXXXXXXXXXXXXX	>	Faial Island	Never Reached Port	
	M-H-022							[Pennsylvania]	[? Sept 1719]		[Portugal]	Distress of Weather	
	S-?-017												
							>	Lisbon	Before 22 Nov 1719				
								[Portugal]					

XXXXXXXXXX XXXXXXXXXX Captain / Master Changed Ships XXXXXXXXXX XXXXXXXXXX

	1721	Isaac & Mary	Sloop				Start	Boston	[20 Apr 1721] XX [11 May 1721] XX XXXXXXXXXXXXXX XXXXXXXXXXXXXX	>	Philadelphia		> M-G-015 / S-I-003 / Page # 69
	S-I-003							[Massachusetts]			[Pennsylvania]		
	5:22 / 6:40												

	1720	Susanna	Sloop		Thomas	Glentworth	Start	Philadelphia	XXXXXXXXXXXXXX XXXXXXXXXXXXXX	>			
	M-G-015							[Pennsylvania]	[14 Jul 1720]		South Carolina		
	S-S-032												
							>	Philadelphia	10 Oct 1720 XXXXXXXXXXXXXX XXXXXXXXXXXXXX				
								[Pennsylvania]					

XXXXXXXXXX XXXXXXXXXX Captain / Master Changed Ships XXXXXXXXXX XXXXXXXXXX

| M-H-022 / S-I-003 / Page # 69 < | 1721 | Isaac & Mary | Sloop | | | | Start | Philadelphia | XX [20 Apr 1721] XX [11 May 1721] XXXXXXXXXXXXXX XXXXXXXXXXXXXX | > | | Never Left For Port | |
| | S-I-003 | | | | | | | [Pennsylvania] | | | South Carolina | See Next Ship Or Captain | |

XXXXXXXXXX XXXXXXXXXX Captain / Master Changed Ships XXXXXXXXXX XXXXXXXXXX

	1721 – 1722	Little Joseph	Sloop	15 Tons			Start	Philadelphia	XXXXXXXXXXXXXX XXXXXXXXXXXXXX [18 May 1721]	>			
	S-L-007	Philadelphia, Pennsylvania						[Pennsylvania]			South Carolina		
							>	Philadelphia	17 Jul 1721 [27 Jul 1721] [3 Aug 1721]	>	Jamaica		> M-H-023 / S-L-007 / Page # 70
								[Pennsylvania]					
							>			>	Philadelphia	[15 Mar 1722] XX [10 May 1722] XX XXXXXXXXXXXXXX XXXXXXXXXXXXXX	
								South Carolina			[Pennsylvania]		

XXXXXXXXXX XXXXXXXXXX Captain / Master Changed Ships XXXXXXXXXX XXXXXXXXXX

	1723	Bonneville	Sloop				Start	Philadelphia	XXXXXXXXXXXXXX [18 Apr 1723] [9 May 1723]	>	Newfoundland		
	S-B-019							[Pennsylvania]					
							>	Philadelphia	[15 Aug 1723] [31 Oct 1723] [29 Nov 1723]	>	Madeira Island		
								[Pennsylvania]			[Portugal]		
	3:115 / 5:75,112 / 6:46,49,53,79,84,87 / 7:32 / 8:40,50,88,118,130							(Sloop / Little Joseph) Philadelphia / Registered – 11 May 1721					

Interact					Captain / Master		Passage	Arrival / Departure 1		Passage	Arrival / Departure 2		Page
26	Year	Name	Type	Burden	First Name	Last Name	Length	Port	Arrival / Entered Inwards; Custom In / Entered Out	Length	Port	Arrival / Entered Inwards; Custom In / Entered Out	**70**
	MSTR ID#	Registry Location						State / Country	Custom Out / Cleared Out; Departure		State / Country	Custom Out / Cleared Out; Departure	
	SHIP ID#												
	Source							Notes					

Entry: Little Joseph

Interact: M-G-015 / S-L-007 / Page # 69 <

Year	Name	Type	Burden	First Name	Last Name	Length	Port	Arr/Dep 1 dates	Length	Port	Arr/Dep 2 dates
1722	Little Joseph	Sloop	15 Tons	Charles	Hargrave	Start	Philadelphia	XX [15 Mar 1722] XX / [10 May 1722] / [24 May 1722]	>	St Christopher's	Never Reached Port / Taken / Pirates
M-H-023	Philadelphia, Pennsylvania						[Pennsylvania]				
S-L-007						&	Taken by Pirates 3 Times / Most of Cargo Taken, Force to Turn Back		>	Philadelphia / [Pennsylvania]	[26 Jul 1722] / XX [25 Oct 1722] XX / XXXXXXXXXXXXXX / XXXXXXXXXXXXXX

Interact (right): > M-J-007 / S-L-007 / Page #71

XXXXXXXXXX XXXXXXXXXX Captain / Master Changed Ships XXXXXXXXXX XXXXXXXXXX

Entry: Salamander

Interact: M-?-000 / S-S-033 / Page # 71 <

Year	Name	Type	First Name	Last Name	Length	Port	Arr/Dep 1 dates	Length	Port	Arr/Dep 2 dates
1722	Salamander	Sloop			Start	Philadelphia	XX [30 Aug 1722] XX / XXXXXXXXXXXXXX / [6 Sept 1722]	>	Boston	XXXXXXXXXXXXXX / XXXXXXXXXXXXXX / XXXXXXXXXXXXXX
S-S-033						[Pennsylvania]			[Massachusetts]	

XXXXXXXXXX XXXXXXXXXX Captain / Master Changed Ships XXXXXXXXXX XXXXXXXXXX

Entry: Boneta

Year	Name	Type	Length	Port	Arr/Dep 1 dates	Length	Port	Arr/Dep 2 dates
1722	Boneta	Sloop	Start	Boston	XXXXXXXXXXXXXX / [8 Oct 1722]	>	Philadelphia	[11 Oct 1722] / [18 Oct 1722] / [25 Oct 1722]
S-B-020				[Massachusetts]			[Pennsylvania]	
			>	Boston / [Massachusetts]	XXXXXXXXXXXXXX / XXXXXXXXXXXXXX / XXXXXXXXXXXXXX			

XXXXXXXXXX XXXXXXXXXX Captain / Master Changed Ships XXXXXXXXXX XXXXXXXXXX

Entry: Endeavor

Year	Name	Type	Length	Port	Arr/Dep 1 dates	Length	Port	Arr/Dep 2 dates
1722 – 1723	Endeavor	Sloop	Start	Boston	XXXXXXXXXXXXXX	>	Philadelphia	[11 Dec 1722]
S-E-011				[Massachusetts]			[Pennsylvania]	[26 Dec 1722]
			>	Boston	[14 Jan 1723]	[>]	Philadelphia	
				[Massachusetts]			[Pennsylvania]	
			>	Boston	[27 Apr 1723]	>	Philadelphia	
				[Massachusetts]	[4 May 1723]		[Pennsylvania]	

Source: 7:54,60,89,90,106,118,120,122,142,148 / 20:62,76,91,92

Entry: Antelope

Interact: M-J-007 / S-A-010 / Page # 71 <

Year	Name	Type	First Name	Last Name	Length	Port	Arr/Dep 1 dates	Length	Port
1722	Antelope	Sloop	Samuel	Bourdet	Start	Philadelphia	XX [17 May 1722] XX / XXXXXXXXXXXXXX / [13 Sept 1722]	>	Antigua
M-B-034						[Pennsylvania]			
S-A-010									

Source: 7:108

Entry: Mary / Judith

Interact: M-J-007 / S-M-029 / Page # 71 <

Year	Name	Type	First Name	Last Name	Length	Port	Arr/Dep 1 dates	Length	Port	Arr/Dep 2 dates
1721	Mary	Sloop	Joseph	Nisbet	Start	Virginia	XXXXXXXXXXXXXX	>	Philadelphia	12 Apr 1721 / XXXXXXXXXXXXXX / XXXXXXXXXXXXXX / XXXXXXXXXXXXXX
M-N-005									[Pennsylvania]	
S-M-029										

XXXXXXXXXX XXXXXXXXXX Captain / Master Changed Ships XXXXXXXXXX XXXXXXXXXX

Year	Name	Type	Length	Port	Arr/Dep 1 dates	Port
1721	Judith	Sloop	>	Philadelphia	XXXXXXXXXXXXXX / [20 Apr 1721] / [27 Apr 1721]	Virginia
S-J-013				[Pennsylvania]		

Source: 6:38,40,42

Notes: (Sloop / Mary) Brought Ship Back From Virginia After It Was Taken By Pirates

Interact	Ship: Year / MSTR ID# / SHIP ID#	Name / Registry Location	Type	Burden	Captain First Name	Captain Last Name	Passage Length	Port / State-Country (A/D 1)	Arrival / Custom / Departure (A/D 1)	Passage Length	Port / State-Country (A/D 2)	Arrival / Custom / Departure (A/D 2) / Notes	Page
26													71

Mary
- 1720 | M-J-007 | S-M-029 | *Mary* | Sloop | Samuel | Jacobs | Start | Philadelphia [Pennsylvania] | [15 Sept 1720] / [15 Sept 1720] | > | Barbados | Never Reached Port / Taken / Spanish Privateer → M-N-005, S-M-029, Page # 70
- > | Delaware Bay | ?? ??? 1720 / Taken / Spanish Privateer | > | Capes of Virginia | XXXXXXXXXXXXXX XXXXXXXXXXXXXX XXXXXXXXXXXXXX

XXXXXXXXXX XXXXXXXXXX Captain / Master Changed Ships XXXXXXXXXX XXXXXXXXXX

Antelope
- 1721 | S-A-010 | *Antelope* | Sloop | Start | Philadelphia [Pennsylvania] | [15 Jun 1721] | > | Barbados
- > | Philadelphia [Pennsylvania] | 25 Aug 1721 / [7 Sept 1721] / [28 Sept 1721] | > | Barbados → M-B-034, S-A-010, Page # 70
- [>] | St Christopher's | > | Philadelphia [Pennsylvania] | [17 May 1722] / XXXXXXXXXXXXXX / XX [13 Sept 1722] XX / XXXXXXXXXXXXXX

XXXXXXXXXX XXXXXXXXXX Captain / Master Changed Ships XXXXXXXXXX XXXXXXXXXX

Little Joseph
- M-H-023, S-L-007, Page # 70 (left reference) | 1722 – 1723 | S-L-007 | *Little Joseph* | Philadelphia, Pennsylvania | Sloop | 15 Tons | Start | Philadelphia [Pennsylvania] | XX [26 Jul 1722] XX / [25 Oct 1722] / [15 Nov 1722] | > | North Carolina
- > | [Philadelphia] [Pennsylvania] | [14 Mar 1723]

Source: 5:99,126 / 6:60,96,100,108 / 7:34,58,122,132 / 8:26

Salamander
- M-D-012, S-S-033, Page # 72 (left reference) | 1722 | M-E-003 | S-S-033 | *Salamander* | Sloop | Cornelius | Empson | Start | Boston [Massachusetts] | XXXXXXXXXXXXXX / [13 Aug 1722] | > | Philadelphia [Pennsylvania] | [30 Aug 1722] / XXXXXXXXXXXXXX / XX [6 Sept 1722] XX / XXXXXXXXXXXXXX → M-H-023, S-S-033, Page # 70

XXXXXXXXXX XXXXXXXXXX Captain / Master Changed Ships XXXXXXXXXX XXXXXXXXXX

Hope
- 1723 | S-H-015 | *Hope* | Brigantine | Start | Boston [Massachusetts] | > | Philadelphia [Pennsylvania] | [7 Mar 1723] / [7 Mar 1723] / [21 Mar 1723]
- > | Barbados [Pennsylvania] | > | Philadelphia | [20 Jun 1723] / [27 Jun 1723] / [4 Jul 1723] → M-D-012, S-H-015, Page # 72
- > | Barbados [Pennsylvania] | > | Philadelphia | [11 Oct 1723] / XX [24 Oct 1723] XX / XXXXXXXXXXXXXX / XXXXXXXXXXXXXX

Source: 7:102 / 8:24,28,68,70,73,112 / 20:54

Interact	Ship				Captain / Master		Passage	Arrival / Departure 1		Passage	Arrival / Departure 2		Page
	Year	Name	Type	Burden	First Name	Last Name	Length	Port	Arrival / Entered Inwards	Length	Port	Arrival / Entered Inwards	
26	MSTR ID#								Custom In / Entered Out			Custom In / Entered Out	72
	SHIP ID#	Registry Location						State / Country	Custom Out / Cleared Out		State / Country	Custom Out / Cleared Out	
	Source								Departure		Notes	Departure	

	1720 – 1722	*Salamander*	Sloop		Barnabas	De Haes	Start	Philadelphia	[24 Nov 1720]	>			
	M-D-012								[1 Dec 1720]				
	S-S-033							[Pennsylvania]			South Carolina		
							>	Philadelphia	[16 Mar 1721]	>			
									[16 Mar 1721]				
								[Pennsylvania]	[23 Mar 1721]		South Carolina		
							>	Philadelphia	[25 May 1721]	>			
								[Pennsylvania]	[8 Jun 1721]		South Carolina		
							>	Philadelphia	8 Aug 1721	>			> M-E-003 S-S-033 Page # 71
									[17 Aug 1721]				
								[Pennsylvania]	[17 Aug 1721]		Virginia		
							>	Philadelphia	[28 Sept 1721]	>	Madeira Island		
									[23 Nov 1721]				
								[Pennsylvania]	[30 Nov 1721]		[Portugal]		
							[>]	Jamaica		>	Philadelphia	[28 Jun 1722]	
												[5 Jul 1722]	
											[Pennsylvania]	[19 Jul 1722]	
							>	Boston	XXXXXXXXXXXXXX				
									XX [13 Aug 1722] XX				
								[Massachusetts]	XXXXXXXXXXXXXX				
	XXXXXXXXXX XXXXXXXXXX Captain / Master Changed Ships XXXXXXXXX XXXXXXXXXX												
M-E-003 S-H-015 < Page # 71	1723	*Hope*	Brigantine				Start	Philadelphia	XX [11 Oct 1723] XX	>	Barbados		
									[24 Oct 1723]				
	S-H-015							[Pennsylvania]	[21 Nov 1723]				
	5:133,136 / 6:28,32,53,58,90,92,108,134,138 / 7:76,79,85 / 8:114,128												

Interact	Ship				Captain / Master		Passage	Arrival / Departure 1			Passage	Arrival / Departure 2			Page
	Year	Name	Type	Burden	First Name	Last Name	Length	Port	Arrival / Entered Inwards		Length	Port	Arrival / Entered Inwards		
27									Custom In / Entered Out				Custom In / Entered Out		73
	MSTR ID#	Registry Location						State / Country	Custom Out / Cleared Out			State / Country	Custom Out / Cleared Out		
	SHIP ID#								Departure				Departure		
		Source							Notes						

1720 – 1721	Margaret	Sloop			Thomas	Read	Start			>	Philadelphia	3 Jun 1720			
M-R-017												[30 Jun 1720]			
S-M-030								Virginia			[Pennsylvania]	[4 Aug 1720]			
							>	Antigua		>	Philadelphia	23 Nov 1720			
												[31 Jan 1721]			
											[Pennsylvania]	[9 Mar 1721]			
							>	Barbados		>					

XXXXXXXXXX XXXXXXXXXX Captain / Master Changed Ships XXXXXXXXXX XXXXXXXXXX

1721	Paradox	Sloop				Start	Philadelphia	XXXXXXXXXXXXXX	>	Barbados			
								XXXXXXXXXXXXXX					
S-P-017							[Pennsylvania]	[27 Jul 1721]					
						>	Philadelphia	16 Nov 1721				M-P-017	
								XX [13 Feb 1722] XX				S-P-017	
							[Pennsylvania]	XXXXXXXXXXXXXX				Page #74	
								XXXXXXXXXXXXXX					

5:60,70,86,133 / 6:14,26,84,132,134

1719	John & Sarah	Sloop			Matthew	Watson	Start	Philadelphia		>	Bermuda		M-W-021
M-W-020													S-J-014
S-J-014							[Pennsylvania]	[29 Dec 1719]					Page # 73

5:4

1720	John & Sarah	Sloop			Matthew	Wooton / Wooten	Start	Providence		>	Philadelphia	[9 Jun 1720]	M-P-017
M-W-021												XX [28 Jul 1720] XX	S-J-014
S-J-014											[Pennsylvania]	XXXXXXXXXXXXXX	Page #74
												XXXXXXXXXXXXXX	

M-W-020 / S-J-014 / Page # 73 <

XXXXXXXXXX XXXXXXXXXX Captain / Master Changed Ships XXXXXXXXXX XXXXXXXXXX

1720	Little Betty	Sloop			Start	Philadelphia	XXXXXXXXXXXXXX	>		Never Left For Port	
							[13 Oct 1720]				
S-L-008	Philadelphia, Pennsylvania					[Pennsylvania]	XXXXXXXXXXXXXX		North Carolina	See Next Ship Or Captain	
							XXXXXXXXXXXXXX				

XXXXXXXXXX Changed Departure Location XXXXXXXXXX

					Start	Philadelphia	XXXXXXXXXXXXXX	>	Jamaica		
							[27 Oct 1720]				
						[Pennsylvania]	[17 Nov 1720]				
					>	Jamaica	After Arrival				
							Taken By Crew				

5:60,112,120,129 / 6:36   (Sloop / Little Betty) - Taken / By Crew & Passengers : Captain Left On Shore

Interact		Ship				Captain / Master		Passage	Arrival / Departure 1		Passage	Arrival / Departure 2		Page
	Year	Name	Type	Burden		First Name	Last Name	Length	Port	Arrival / Entered Inwards / Custom In / Entered Out / Custom Out / Cleared Out / Departure	Length	Port	Arrival / Entered Inwards / Custom In / Entered Out / Custom Out / Cleared Out / Departure	
27	MSTR ID#								State / Country			State / Country		**74**
	SHIP ID#	Registry Location												
				Source						Notes				

		1719	*Diligence*	Sloop		James	Peartree	Start	Philadelphia		>	Lisbon	Arrived Before 22 Nov 1719]	
	M-P-017													
	S-D-012								[Pennsylvania]			[Portugal]		

XXXXXXXXX XXXXXXXXXX Captain / Master Changed Ships XXXXXXXXX XXXXXXXXXX

	1720 – 1721	*John & Sarah*	Sloop				Start	Philadelphia	XX [9 Jun 1720] XX [28 Jul 1720] [11 Aug 1720]	>	Antigua	
	S-J-014							[Pennsylvania]				
M-W-021							>	Philadelphia	22 Nov 1720 [1 Dec 1720] [13 Dec 1720]	>	Barbados	
S-J-014								[Pennsylvania]				
Page # 73							>	Philadelphia	1 May 1721 [25 May 1721] XXXXXXXXXXXXXX XXXXXXXXXXXXXX	>	St Christopher's	Never Left For Port / See Next Ship Or Captain
								[Pennsylvania]				

XXXXXXXXX XXXXXXXXXX Captain / Master Changed Ships XXXXXXXXX XXXXXXXXXX

	1721	*Lincoln-shire*	Sloop				Start	Philadelphia	XXXXXXXXXXXXXX XXXXXXXXXXXXXX [8 Jun 1721]	>	St Christopher's	
	S-L-009							[Pennsylvania]				
							[>]	Antigua		>	Philadelphia	[5 Oct 1721] XX [19 Dec 1721] XX XXXXXXXXXXXXXX XXXXXXXXXXXXXX
											[Pennsylvania]	

> M-G-016 / S-L-009 / Page # 77

XXXXXXXXX XXXXXXXXXX Captain / Master Changed Ships XXXXXXXXX XXXXXXXXXX

	1722	*Paradox*	Sloop				Start	Philadelphia	XX [16 Nov 1721] XX [13 Feb 1722] [20 Feb 1722]	>	South Carolina	
M-R-017	S-P-017							[Pennsylvania]				
S-P-017							>	Philadelphia	[10 May 1722] XX [24 May 1722] XX XXXXXXXXXXXXXX XXXXXXXXXXXXXX			
Page # 73								[Pennsylvania]				

> M-H-024 / S-P-017 / Page # 74

XXXXXXXXX XXXXXXXXXX Captain / Master Changed Ships XXXXXXXXX XXXXXXXXXX

	1723						>	Faial Island		>	Boston	[13 Apr 1723]
	S-?-018							[Portugal]			[Massachusetts]	[24 Aug 1723]
							>	New Hampshire				

5:22,82,88,133,136,141 / 6:44,53,58,112 / 7:16,20,54 / 20:89,108

	1722	*Paradox*	Sloop		Thomas	Hopper	Start	Philadelphia	XX [10 May 1722] XX [24 May 1722] [14 Jun 1722]	>	Antigua	
M-P-017	M-H-024							[Pennsylvania]				
S-P-017	S-P-017											
Page # 74				7:60,70								

> M-C-016 / S-P-017 / Page # 75

Interact	Ship				Captain / Master		Passage	Arrival / Departure 1		Passage	Arrival / Departure 2		Page
	Year	Name	Type	Burden	First Name	Last Name	Length	Port	Arrival / Entered Inwards	Length	Port	Arrival / Entered Inwards	
27									Custom In / Entered Out			Custom In / Entered Out	75
	MSTR ID#								Custom Out / Cleared Out			Custom Out / Cleared Out	
	SHIP ID#	Registry Location						State / Country	Departure		State / Country	Departure	
	Source							Notes					

	1722	*Paradox*	Sloop		Thomas	Carpenter	Start	Burlington		>	Philadelphia	[18 Oct 1722]	
												[18 Oct 1722]	
M-H-024	M-C-016							[New Jersey]			[Pennsylvania]	[1 Nov 1722]	
S-P-017	S-P-017						>	Antigua					
Page # 74													

XXXXXXXXXX XXXXXXXXXX Captain / Master Changed Ships XXXXXXXXXX XXXXXXXXXX

	1723	*Loyal Burnett*	Sloop				Start	Philadelphia	XX [30 May 1723] XX	>	Jamaica		
M-P-018									XXXXXXXXXXXXXXX				
S-I-010	S-L-010							[Pennsylvania]	[27 Jun 1723]				
Page # 77	7:120,126 / 8:70												

	1720	*St Peter*	Snow		Owen	Meredith	Start	Madeira Island		>	Philadelphia	[7 Apr 1720]	
												[12 May 1720]	
	M-M-013							[Portugal]			[Pennsylvania]	[23 Jun 1720]	
	S-S-034						>	Madeira Island					
								[Portugal]					

XXXXXXXXXX XXXXXXXXXX Captain / Master Changed Ships XXXXXXXXXX XXXXXXXXXX

	1721 – 1722	*Loyal Burnett*	Sloop				Start	Philadelphia	[18 May 1721]	>	Barbados		
									[21 Jun 1721]				
	S-L-010							[Pennsylvania]					
							>	Anguilla		>	Philadelphia	[19 Oct 1721]	
												[13 Feb 1722]	
											[Pennsylvania]	[29 Mar 1722]	
							>	Barbados		[>]	Antigua		M-S-029
													S-L-010
													Page # 76
							>	Philadelphia	[6 Sept 1722]				
									XX [10 Oct 1722] XX				
								[Pennsylvania]	XX [8 Nov 1722] XX				
									XXXXXXXXXXXXXXX				
	5:34,50,67 / 6:49,63,120 / 7:16,38,106												

Interact	Ship				Captain / Master		Passage	Arrival / Departure 1		Passage	Arrival / Departure 2		Page
	Year	Name	Type	Burden	First Name	Last Name	Length	Port	Arrival / Entered Inwards	Length	Port	Arrival / Entered Inwards	
27									Custom In / Entered Out			Custom In / Entered Out	76
	MSTR ID#							State / Country	Custom Out / Cleared Out		State / Country	Custom Out / Cleared Out	
	SHIP ID#	Registry Location							Departure			Departure	
	Source							Notes					

	1720 – 1721	Olive Branch	Sloop		Thomas	Stockin / Stocken	Start	Barbados		>	Philadelphia	15 Jul 1720
												[11 Aug 1720]
	M-S-029										[Pennsylvania]	[18 Aug 1720]
	S-O-003											
							>	Barbados		>	Philadelphia	15 Nov 1720
												[17 Jan 1721]
											[Pennsylvania]	[7 Feb 1721]
							>	Barbados		>	Philadelphia	26 May 1721
												[8 Jun 1721]
											[Pennsylvania]	[21 Jun 1721]
							>	Jamaica		>	Philadelphia	[19 Oct 1721]
												[16 Nov 1721]
											[Pennsylvania]	[30 Nov 1721]
							>	Madeira Island				
								[Portugal]				

XXXXXXXXXX XXXXXXXXXX Captain / Master Changed Ships XXXXXXXXXX XXXXXXXXXX

	1722	Loyal Burnett	Sloop				Start	Philadelphia	XXXXXXXXXXXXXX	>	Jamaica	Never Left For Port
									[3 Oct 1722]			
	S-L-010							[Pennsylvania]	XXXXXXXXXXXXXX			See Next Ship Or Captain
									XXXXXXXXXXXXXX			

M-M-013
S-I-010
Page # 75

XXXXXXXXXX Changed Departure Location XXXXXXXXXX

M-P-018
S-L-010
Page # 77

							Start	Philadelphia	XXXXXXXXXXXXXX	>	Madeira Island	Never Left For Port
									[10 Oct 1722]			
								[Pennsylvania]	XX [8 Nov 1722] XX		[Portugal]	See Next Ship Or Captain
									XXXXXXXXXXXXXX			

XXXXXXXXXX XXXXXXXXXX Captain / Master Changed Ships XXXXXXXXXX XXXXXXXXXX

	1723	Carpenter	Sloop				Start	Philadelphia	XX [14 Mar 1723] XX	>	Madeira Island	
									[4 Apr 1723]			
	S-C-015							[Pennsylvania]	[18 Apr 1723]		[Portugal]	
							[>]	Barbados		>	Philadelphia	[22 Aug 1723]
												[29 Aug 1723]
											[Pennsylvania]	[6 Sept 1723]
							>	Madeira Island				
								[Portugal]				

M-W-022
S-C-015
Page #79

5:78,88,90,129 / 6:10,16,56,58,63,120,132,138 / 7:114 / 8:34,40,91,96

Interact					Captain / Master		Passage	Arrival / Departure 1		Passage	Arrival / Departure 2		Page
	Ship							Port	Arrival / Entered Inwards		Port	Arrival / Entered Inwards	
	Year	Name	Type	Burden	First Name	Last Name	Length		Custom In / Entered Out	Length		Custom In / Entered Out	77
27	MSTR ID#							State / Country	Custom Out / Cleared Out		State / Country	Custom Out / Cleared Out	
	SHIP ID#	Registry Location							Departure			Departure	
	Source							Notes					

Entry 1:

M-S-029 / S-I-010 / Page # 76	1722 – 1723 M-P-018 S-L-010	Loyal Burnett Sloop	Matthew Phillips	Start	Philadelphia [Pennsylvania]	XX [6 Sept 1722] XX / XX [10 Oct 1722] XX / [8 Nov 1722]	> Madeira Island [Portugal]	M-C-016 / S-L-010 / Page # 75

| | | [>] | Antigua | > | Philadelphia [Pennsylvania] | [30 May 1723] / XXXXXXXXXXXXX / XX [27 Jun 1723] XX / XXXXXXXXXXXXX |

XXXXXXXXXX XXXXXXXXXX Captain / Master Changed Ships XXXXXXXXXX XXXXXXXXXX

| 1723 S-S-035 | Samuel & Anne Snow | Start | Philadelphia [Pennsylvania] | XXXXXXXXXXXXX / [26 Sept 1723] / [7 Nov 1723] | > Barbados |

7:130 / 8:60,103,122

Entry 2:

M-P-017 / S-L-009 / Page # 74	1721 – 1722 M-G-016 S-L-009	Lincoln-shire Sloop	Edward Greenman	Start	Philadelphia [Pennsylvania]	XX [5 Oct 1721] XX / [19 Dec 1721] / [6 Feb 1722]	> Antigua	M-S-030 / S-L-009 / Page # 78

| | | > | Philadelphia [Pennsylvania] | [24 May 1722] / XXXXXXXXXXXXX / XX [21 Jun 1722] XX / XXXXXXXXXXXXX |

XXXXXXXXXX XXXXXXXXXX Captain / Master Changed Ships XXXXXXXXXX XXXXXXXXXX

| 1722 – 1723 S-H-016 | Hopeful Betty Sloop | Start | Philadelphia [Pennsylvania] | XXXXXXXXXXXXX / XXXXXXXXXXXXX / [29 Nov 1722] | > Suriname | | 4 Mar 1723 |

| | | > | Philadelphia [Pennsylvania] | [4 Apr 1723] / [25 Apr 1723] | > Suriname | Never Reached Port / Taken / Pirates |

| | | > | Capes of Delaware | 5 Jun 1723 / Taken / Pirates | > Philadelphia [Pennsylvania] | 12 Jun 1723 |

| | | [>] | Suriname | | > Philadelphia [Pennsylvania] | [3 Oct 1723] / [28 Nov 1723] / [9 Dec 1723] |

| | | > | Suriname | | | |

6:146 / 7:13,60,138 / 8:34,42,65,118,130,134

Interact		Ship				Captain / Master		Passage		Arrival / Departure 1		Passage		Arrival / Departure 2		Page
	Year	Name	Type	Burden		First Name	Last Name	Length	Port	Arrival / Entered Inwards / Custom In / Entered Out	Length		Port	Arrival / Entered Inwards / Custom In / Entered Out		
27	MSTR ID#									Custom Out / Cleared Out				Custom Out / Cleared Out		78
	SHIP ID#	Registry Location							State / Country	Departure			State / Country	Departure		
		Source								Notes						

M-G-016 < S-L-009 Page # 77	1722 – 1723 M-S-030 S-L-009	Lincoln-shire	Sloop		George	Slyfield	Start	Philadelphia [Pennsylvania]	XX [24 May 1722] XX XXXXXXXXXXXXXX [21 Jun 1722]	>	Suriname			> M-M-014 S-L-009 Page # 78
				Start				Philadelphia [Pennsylvania]	[27 Sept 1722] [15 Nov 1722] [29 Nov 1722]	>	Madeira Island [Portugal]		
				[>]				Antigua		>	Philadelphia [Pennsylvania]	[16 May 1723] [30 May 1723]	
				>				South Carolina		>	Philadelphia [Pennsylvania]	[29 Jul 1723] [15 Aug 1723] [6 Sept 1723]	
				>				South Carolina		>	Philadelphia [Pennsylvania]	[14 Nov 1723] XX [28 Nov 1723] XX XXXXXXXXXXXXXX XXXXXXXXXXXXXX	

Source (row 1): 7:74,112,132,138 / 8:54,60,62,84,88,91,96,126

| M-S-030 < S-L-009 Page # 78 | 1723 M-M-014 S-L-009 | Lincoln-shire | Sloop | | Thomas | Munford | Start | Philadelphia [Pennsylvania] | XXXXXXXXXXXXXX [28 Nov 1723] XX [17 Dec 1723] XX XXXXXXXXXXXXXX | > | Antigua | Never Left For Port See Next Ship Or Captain | | > M-B-035 S-L-009 Page # 78 |

Source: 8:130

| M-M-014 < S-L-009 Page # 78 | 1723 M-B-035 S-L-009 | Lincoln-shire | Sloop | | Robert | Bird | Start | Philadelphia [Pennsylvania] | XXXXXXXXXXXXXX XX [28 Nov 1723] XX [17 Dec 1723] | > | Antigua | | | |

Source: 8:136

Interact	Ship				Captain / Master		Passage	Arrival / Departure 1		Passage	Arrival / Departure 2		Page
	Year	Name	Type	Burden	First Name	Last Name	Length	Port	Arrival / Entered Inwards / Custom In / Entered Out / Custom Out / Cleared Out / Departure	Length	Port	Arrival / Entered Inwards / Custom In / Entered Out / Custom Out / Cleared Out / Departure	
27	MSTR ID#	Registry Location						State / Country			State / Country		79
	SHIP ID#											Notes	
	Source												

Row group 1

- Year: 1720 – 1722 | Name: *Endeavor* | Type: Sloop | MSTR ID#: M-W-022 | SHIP ID#: S-E-012
- Captain / Master: William Wallace

Passage Length	Port	Dates	Passage Length	Port	Dates	Link
Start	Philadelphia / [Pennsylvania]	[13 Oct 1720] / [17 Nov 1720]	>	York River / Virginia		
>	Philadelphia / [Pennsylvania]	24 Feb 1721 / [2 Mar 1721] / [9 Mar 1721]	>	Antigua		
[>]	Bristol / [England]		>	Philadelphia / [Pennsylvania]	[5 Oct 1721] / [2 Nov 1721] / [16 Nov 1721]	> M-T-012 / S-E-012 / Page # 79
>	South Carolina				NO SUPPORTING DATA TO LINK TIMELINE	
Start	Antigua		>	Philadelphia / [Pennsylvania]	[18 Dec 1722] / XX [14 Jan 1723] XX / XXXXXXXXXXXXX / XXXXXXXXXXXXX	

XXXXXXXXX XXXXXXXXX Captain / Master Changed Ships XXXXXXXXX XXXXXXXXX

- Year: 1723 | Name: *Carpenter* | Type: Sloop | SHIP ID#: S-C-015

Passage Length	Port	Port	Dates	Link
Start	Maryland	[Philadelphia] / [Pennsylvania]	[14 Mar 1723] / XX [4 Apr 1723] XX / XXXXXXXXXXXXX / XXXXXXXXXXXXX	> M-S-029 / S-C-015 / Page # 76

Source: 5:112,129 / 6:23,26,112,125,132 / 7:146 / 8:26

Row group 2

- Year: 1723 | Name: *Endeavor* | Type: Sloop | MSTR ID#: M-T-012 | SHIP ID#: S-E-012
- Captain / Master: Joseph Turner
- Link (left): M-W-022 / S-E-012 / Page # 79 <

Passage Length	Port	Dates	Passage Length	Port	Dates
Start	[Philadelphia] / [Pennsylvania]	XX [18 Dec 1722] XX / [14 Jan 1723] / [22 Jan 1723]	>	Antigua	
[>]	Maryland		>	Philadelphia / [Pennsylvania]	[23 May 1723] / [23 May 1723] / [30 May 1723]
>	Antigua				

Source: 8:6,8,58,60

Interact	Ship				Captain / Master		Passage	Arrival / Departure 1		Passage	Arrival / Departure 2		Page
	Year	Name	Type	Burden	First Name	Last Name	Length	Port	Arrival / Entered Inwards / Custom In / Entered Out	Length	Port	Arrival / Entered Inwards / Custom In / Entered Out	
28	MSTR ID#								Custom Out / Cleared Out			Custom Out / Cleared Out	80
	SHIP ID#	Registry Location						State / Country	Departure		State / Country	Departure	
	Source							Notes					

Entry 1
1720	Caesar	Brigantine		David	Burch	Start	London		>	Philadelphia	31 Aug 1720 / XX [20 Oct 1720] XX / XXXXXXXXXXXXXX	M-M-003
M-B-036												S-C-017
S-C-017							[England]	8 Jul 1720		[Pennsylvania]	XXXXXXXXXXXXXX	Page # 80
Source: 5:94												

Entry 2
Interact: M-B-036 / S-C-017 / Page # 80

1720	Caesar	Brigantine		John	Moorecraft	Start	Philadelphia	XX 31 Aug 1720 XX / [20 Oct 1720] / [27 Oct 1720]	>	Wye River		M-L-010
M-M-003												S-C-017
S-C-017							[Pennsylvania]			Maryland		Page # 80
Source: 5:115,120												

Entry 3
Interact: M-M-003 / S-C-017 / Page # 80

1721	Caesar	Brigantine		William	Lea / Lee	Start	Holland		>	Dartmouth [England]		M-G-017
M-L-010												S-C-017
S-C-017												Page # 80
						>	Philadelphia	15 Sept 1721 / [16 Nov 1721] / XX [29 Mar 1722] XX / XXXXXXXXXXXXXX	>	Antigua	Never Left For Port / See Next Ship Or Captain	
							[Pennsylvania]					

XXXXXXXXXX XXXXXXXXX Captain / Master Changed Ships XXXXXXXXX XXXXXXXXXX

Entry 4
Interact: M-M-015 / S-R-008 / Page # 82

1723	Richard & Elizabeth	Sloop				Start	Philadelphia	XX [26 Sept 1723] XX / [17 Oct 1723] / [24 Oct 1723]	>			
S-R-008							[Pennsylvania]			Virginia		
Source: 6:106,132 / 8:112,114							(Known Passengers / Palatine) Philadelphia / Inward –15 Sept 1721 – Count 140+					

Entry 5
Interact: M-L-010 / S-C-017 / Page # 80

1722	Caesar	Brigantine		George	Grigg	Start	Philadelphia	XXXXXXXXXXXXXX / XX [16 Nov 1721] XX / [29 Mar 1722]	>	Antigua		M-A-012
M-G-017												S-C-017
S-C-017							[Pennsylvania]					Page # 80
Source: 7:38												

Entry 6
1721	Carpenter	Sloop		Robert	Abbot	Start	Philadelphia	[13 Apr 1721] / [27 Apr 1721]	>	Barbados		
M-A-012							[Pennsylvania]					
S-C-016												
						>	Philadelphia	24 Jul 1721 / [3 Aug 1721] / [31 Aug 1721]	>	Barbados		M-D-013
							[Pennsylvania]					S-C-016
												Page # 81
						>	Philadelphia	[7 Dec 1721] / XX [29 Mar 1722] XX / XXXXXXXXXXXXXX / XXXXXXXXXXXXXX				
							[Pennsylvania]					

XXXXXXXXXX XXXXXXXXX Captain / Master Changed Ships XXXXXXXXX XXXXXXXXXX

Entry 7
Interact: M-G-017 / S-C-017 / Page # 80

1723	Caesar	Brigantine				>	Dover	[6 Sept 1723] / [17 Oct 1723] / XX [5 Dec 1723] XX / XXXXXXXXXXXXXX	>	Philadelphia		M-N-006
S-C-017							[England]			[Pennsylvania]		S-C-017
												Page # 81
						>	West Indies	Never Left For Port / See Next Ship Or Captain				
Source: 6:34,38,42,84,87,96,140 / 8:96,112												

Interact	Year / MSTR ID# / SHIP ID#	Ship Name	Type	Burden	First Name	Last Name	Passage Length	Port / State-Country	Arrival / Custom In / Custom Out / Departure	Passage Length	Port / State-Country	Arrival / Custom In / Custom Out / Departure	Page
28													81

Interact — Ship — Captain / Master — Passage — Arrival / Departure 1 — Passage — Arrival / Departure 2 — Page

Year — Name — Type — Burden — First Name — Last Name — Length — Port — Arrival / Entered Inwards — Length — Port — Arrival / Entered Inwards

MSTR ID# — Registry Location — Custom In / Entered Out — Custom In / Entered Out

SHIP ID# — State / Country — Custom Out / Cleared Out — State / Country — Custom Out / Cleared Out

Source — Departure — Notes — Departure

Row 1

	1719 – 1720	Bon-Adventure	Snow		Samuel	Naylor	Start	Philadelphia [Pennsylvania]	[22 Dec 1719]	>	Madeira Island [Portugal]	
	M-N-006											
	S-B-021						[>]	Barbados		>	Philadelphia [Pennsylvania]	6 Jul 1720 / [4 Aug 1720] / [29 Sept 1720]
							>	London [England]				

XXXXXXXXXX XXXXXXXXXX Captain / Master Changed Ships XXXXXXXXXX XXXXXXXXXX

| M-A-012 / S-C-017 / Page # 80 | 1723 | Caesar | Brigantine | | | | Start | Philadelphia [Pennsylvania] | XXXXXXXXXXXXXX / XX [17 Oct 1723] XX / [5 Dec 1723] | > | Antigua | |
| | S-C-017 | | | | | | | | | | | |

Source: 5:2,72,86,107 / 8:132

Row 2

	1720 – 1721	Susanna	Sloop		William	Drason	Start	Philadelphia [Pennsylvania]	[2 Feb 1720] / [1 Mar 1720]	>	Suriname	
	M-D-013											
	S-S-036						>	Philadelphia [Pennsylvania]	5 Jul 1720 / [28 Jul 1720] / [18 Aug 1720]	>	Barbados	
							>	Philadelphia [Pennsylvania]	21 Nov 1720 / [17 Jan 1721] / [14 Feb 1721]	>	Suriname	
							>	Philadelphia [Pennsylvania]	15 Jun 1721 / [6 Jul 1721] / [27 Jul 1721]	>	Suriname	
							>	Philadelphia [Pennsylvania]	[7 Dec 1721] / XXXXXXXXXXXXXX / XXXXXXXXXXXXXX / XXXXXXXXXXXXXX			

XXXXXXXXXX XXXXXXXXXX Captain / Master Changed Ships XXXXXXXXXX XXXXXXXXXX

| M-A-012 / S-C-016 / Page # 80 | 1722 | Carpenter | Sloop | | | | > | Philadelphia [Pennsylvania] | XX [7 Dec 1721] XX / [29 Mar 1722] / XX [5 Apr 1722] XX / XXXXXXXXXXXXXX | > | South Carolina | Never Left For Port / See Next Ship Or Captain | M-P-019 / S-C-016 / Page # 83 |
| | S-C-016 | | | | | | | | | | | |

XXXXXXXXXX XXXXXXXXXX Captain / Master Relieved And Then Retook Command XXXXXXXXXX XXXXXXXXXX

| M-P-019 / S-C-016 / Page # 83 | 1722 | Carpenter | Sloop | | | | > | Philadelphia [Pennsylvania] | XX [7 Jun 1722] XX / [21 Jun 1722] / [5 Jul 1722] | > | Antigua | |
| | S-C-016 | | | | | | | | | | | |

Source: 5:14,22,72,82,90,133 / 6:10,18,63,71,84,122,140 / 7:38,74,79

Interact	Ship				Captain / Master		Passage	Arrival / Departure 1				Passage	Arrival / Departure 2		Page
	Year	Name	Type	Burden	First Name	Last Name	Length	Port	Arrival / Entered Inwards / Custom In / Entered Out			Length	Port	Arrival / Entered Inwards / Custom In / Entered Out	
28	MSTR ID# / SHIP ID#	Registry Location						State / Country	Custom Out / Cleared Out / Departure				State / Country	Custom Out / Cleared Out / Departure	82
	Source							Notes								

Sarah (Ship) — M-V-005 / S-S-037 — 1722
- Captain/Master: Bartholomew Vokes
- Passage: Start
- Arrival/Departure 1: Madeira Island [Portugal] — XXXXXXXXXXXXXX — 10 Feb 1722
- Passage: >
- Arrival/Departure 2: Philadelphia [Pennsylvania] — 23 Mar 1722 / [12 Apr 1722] / [19 Apr 1722]

(M-P-019 / S-S-037 / Page # 83 <)
- Madeira Island [Portugal] > Philadelphia [Pennsylvania] — [9 Aug 1722] / [16 Aug 1722] / [6 Sept 1722]
- Madeira Island [Portugal] >
- Source: 7:38,42,46,94,96,106

Mary (Ship) — M-B-037 / S-M-031 — 1720
- Captain/Master: William Bevan
- Passage: Start
- Arrival/Departure 1: Philadelphia [Pennsylvania] — XX 27 Apr 1720 XX / [16 Jun 1720] / [23 Jun 1720]
- Passage: >
- Arrival/Departure 2: Maryland

(M-P-019 / S-M-031 / Page # 83 <)
- Source: 5:63,67

Abigail (Brigantine) — M-C-017 / S-A-012 — 1720
- Captain/Master: William Clunn
- Passage: Start
- Arrival/Departure 1: Barbados
- Passage: >
- Arrival/Departure 2: Antigua

(> M-H-026 / S-A-012 / Page # 82)
- Philadelphia [Pennsylvania] — 14 Aug 1720 / [6 Oct 1720] / XX [10 Nov 1720] XX / XXXXXXXXXXXXXX
- > Barbados — Never Left For Port / See Next Ship Or Captain
- Source: 5:90,110

Ann (Sloop) — M-H-026 / S-A-013 — 1720
- Captain/Master: Isaac Huworth / Howarth
- Passage: Start
- Arrival/Departure 1: Philadelphia [Pennsylvania] — [16 Jun 1720]
- Passage: >
- Arrival/Departure 2: Barbados

(> M-S-031 / S-A-013 / Page # 84)
- Philadelphia [Pennsylvania] — 30 Aug 1720 / XXXXXXXXXXXXXX / XX [15 Sept 1720] XX / XXXXXXXXXXXXXX
- >

XXXXXXXXXX XXXXXXXXXX Captain / Master Changed Ships XXXXXXXXXX XXXXXXXXXX

Abigail (Brigantine) — S-A-012 — 1720
- Passage: Start
- Arrival/Departure 1: Philadelphia [Pennsylvania] — XXXXXXXXXXXXXX / XX [6 Oct 1720] XX / [10 Nov 1720]
- Passage: >
- Arrival/Departure 2: Barbados

(M-C-017 / S-A-012 / Page # 82 <)
- Source: 5:63,94,126

Richard & Elizabeth (Sloop) — M-M-015 / S-R-008 — 1723
- Captain/Master: William Manning
- Passage: Start
- Arrival/Departure 1: Bermuda
- Passage: >
- Arrival/Departure 2: Philadelphia [Pennsylvania] — [26 Sept 1723] / XX [17 Oct 1723] XX / XXXXXXXXXXXXXX / XXXXXXXXXXXXXX

(> M-L-010 / S-R-008 / Page # 80)
- Source: 8:103

Interact	Year	Ship Name	Type	Burden	First Name	Last Name	Passage Length	Port / State-Country	Arrival/Entered Inwards · Custom In/Entered Out · Custom Out/Cleared Out · Departure	Passage Length	Port / State-Country	Arrival/Entered Inwards · Custom In/Entered Out · Custom Out/Cleared Out · Departure / Notes	Page
28													**83**
	1720 · M-P-019 · S-M-031	Mary	Ship		John	Parker	Start	London · [England]		>	Philadelphia · [Pennsylvania]	27 Apr 1720 · XX [16 Jun 1720] XX · XXXXXXXXXXXXXX · XXXXXXXXXXXXXX	> M-B-037 · S-M-031 · Page # 82
— XXXXXXXXX XXXXXXXXX Captain / Master Changed Ships XXXXXXXXX XXXXXXXXX													
	1720 – 1722 · S-S-037	Sarah	Ship				>	Philadelphia · [Pennsylvania]	XXXXXXXXXXXXXX · [19 May 1720] · [23 Jun 1720]	>	Cowes · [England]		
							>	Holland		>	Cowes · [England]		
							>	Philadelphia · [Pennsylvania]	[20 Apr 1721] · [11 May 1721] · [1 Jun 1721]	>	Madeira Island · [Portugal]		> M-V-005 · S-S-037 · Page # 82
							>	Philadelphia · [Pennsylvania]	[2 Nov 1721] · [16 Nov 1721] · [30 Nov 1721]	>	Madeira Island · [Portugal]	XXXXXXXXXXXXXX · XXXXXXXXXXXXXX · XX [10 Feb 1722] XX	
							>	Philadelphia · [Pennsylvania]	Arrived On The Ship Sarah 23 Mar 1722 · New Master Cpt Vokes				
— XXXXXXXXX XXXXXXXXX Captain / Master Changed Ships XXXXXXXXX XXXXXXXXX													
M-D-013 · S-C-016 · Page # 81 <	1722 · S-C-016	Carpenter	Sloop				>	Philadelphia · [Pennsylvania]	XXXXXXXXXXXXXX · XX [29 Mar 1722] XX · [5 Apr 1722]	>	South Carolina		
							>	Philadelphia · [Pennsylvania]	[7 Jun 1722] · XX [21 Jun 1722] XX · XXXXXXXXXXXXXX · XXXXXXXXXXXXXX	>			> M-D-013 · S-C-016 · Page # 82
— XXXXXXXXX XXXXXXXXX Captain / Master Changed Ships XXXXXXXXX XXXXXXXXX													
	1722 · S-H-017	Henry	Snow				>	Philadelphia · [Pennsylvania]	XXXXXXXXXXXXXX · [11 Oct 1722] · XX [8 Nov 1722] XX · XXXXXXXXXXXXXX	>	Madeira Island · [Portugal]	Never Left For Port · See Next Ship Or Captain	> M-S-032 · S-H-017 · Page # 87
— XXXXXXXXX XXXXXXXXX Captain / Master Relieved And Then Retook Command XXXXXXXXX XXXXXXXXX													
	1723 · S-H-017	Henry	Snow				>	Philadelphia · [Pennsylvania]	XX [16 May 1723] XX · XXXXXXXXXXXXXX · [27 Jun 1723]	>	Madeira Island · [Portugal]		
M-S-032 · S-H-017 · Page # 87 <							>	Lisbon · [Portugal]		>		Before 13 Oct 1723 – Plundered by Algerine Rover · Off of the Bar of Lisbon	
							>	Holland					

5:41,45,53,67 / 6:38,40,46,56,125,132,138 / 7:38,40,68,118 / 8:70,130

Interact	Ship				Captain / Master		Passage	Arrival / Departure 1		Passage	Arrival / Departure 2		Page
	Year	Name	Type	Burden	First Name	Last Name	Length	Port	Arrival / Entered Inwards	Length	Port	Arrival / Entered Inwards	
28	MSTR ID#								Custom In / Entered Out			Custom In / Entered Out	84
	SHIP ID#	Registry Location						State / Country	Custom Out / Cleared Out		State / Country	Custom Out / Cleared Out	
									Departure			Departure	
	Source							Notes					

1719	*Unity*	Sloop		Henry	Stevens	Start	Jamaica		>	Philadelphia	[22 Dec 1719]		
M-S-031											XXXXXXXXXXXXXXXX		> M-H-026
S-U-001										[Pennsylvania]	XX [29 Dec 1719] XX		S-U-001
											XXXXXXXXXXXXXXXX		Page # 86

XXXXXXXXXX XXXXXXXXXX Captain / Master Changed Ships XXXXXXXXXX XXXXXXXXXX

1720 – 1721	*Ann*	Sloop				Start	Philadelphia	XX [30 Aug 1720] XX XXXXXXXXXXXXXXXX	>	Antigua			
S-A-013							[Pennsylvania]	[15 Sept 1720]					

M-H-026 < S-A-013 < Page # 82

						>	Philadelphia	2 Dec 1720	>	Barbados			
							[Pennsylvania]	[6 Apr 1721]					
						>	Philadelphia	17 Jul 1721 [27 Jul 1721]	>	Jamaica			
							[Pennsylvania]	[17 Aug 1721]					

5:2,99,138 / 6:36,79,84,92

1720 – 1721	*Rebekah*	Sloop		Joseph	Parker	Start	Antigua		>	Philadelphia	[7 Apr 1720]		
M-P-020													
S-R-009										[Pennsylvania]			
						>	Burlington		>	Antigua			
							[New Jersey]	[26 Apr 1720]					
						>	Philadelphia	18 Aug 1720					
							[Pennsylvania]						

NO SUPPORTING DATA TO LINK TIMELINE

						Start	Antigua		>	Philadelphia	[16 Mar 1721] [30 Mar 1721]		> M-L-012
										[Pennsylvania]	[13 Apr 1721]		S-R-009
													Page # 85
						>	Boston						
							[Massachusetts]						

NO SUPPORTING DATA TO LINK TIMELINE

						Start	Barbados		>	Philadelphia	28 Aug 1721		
										[Pennsylvania]	[5 Oct 1721]		
						>	Barbados						

5:34,41,90 / 6:28,34,36,38,96,112

Interact		Ship				Captain / Master		Passage	Arrival / Departure 1		Passage	Arrival / Departure 2		Page
28	Year	Name	Type	Burden	First Name	Last Name	Length	Port	Arrival / Entered Inwards / Custom In / Entered Out	Length	Port	Arrival / Entered Inwards / Custom In / Entered Out	85
	MSTR ID#								Custom Out / Cleared Out			Custom Out / Cleared Out	
	SHIP ID#	Registry Location						State / Country	Departure		State / Country	Departure	
		Source							Notes				

	1721	*Adventure*	Sloop		Joseph	Lusher	Start	Philadelphia	[5 Oct 1721]	>	Bermuda		
	M-L-012								[24 Oct 1721]				
	S-A-013							[Pennsylvania]					

XXXXXXXXXX XXXXXXXXXX Captain / Master Changed Ships XXXXXXXXXX XXXXXXXXXX

	1722 – 1723	*Rebekah*	Sloop				Start	Turks Island		>	Philadelphia	[26 Apr 1722] / [10 May 1722]	
												[24 May 1722]	
	S-R-009										[Pennsylvania]		
							>	Bermuda		[>]	Philadelphia	[25 Oct 1722]	
											[Pennsylvania]	[23 Nov 1722]	
M-P-020							>	Antigua		>	Philadelphia	[21 Mar 1723]	
S-R-009											[Pennsylvania]	[18 Apr 1723]	
Page # 84							>	Bermuda		>	Philadelphia	[18 Jul 1723] / [25 Jul 1723]	
											[Pennsylvania]	[8 Aug 1723]	
							>	Bermuda					
		6:112,122 / 7:48,54,60,122,136 / 8:28,40,78,81,86											

	1720	*Glasgow*	Sloop		William	Argent	Start	Barbados		>	Bar of Carolina	3 May 1720	
	M-A-013											Taken / Spanish Privateer	
	S-G-008												M-W-024
							>	Bar of Carolina	3 May 1720	>		Never Reached Port	S-G-008
									Took On Board Spanish Privateer Sloop		Carolina	Taken / Spanish Privateer	Page # 85
		5:58							(Sloop / Glasgow) Captain Taken Prisoner – Mate Took Command				

	1720	*Glasgow*	Sloop		William	Warden	Start	Bar of Carolina	10 May 1720	>	Philadelphia	31 May 1720 / [28 Jul 1720]	
	M-W-024								Retaken / Spanish Privateer		[Pennsylvania]	[11 Aug 1720]	
M-A-013	S-G-008												M-H-026
S-G-008							>	Madeira Island					S-G-008
Page # 85								[Portugal]					Page # 86

XXXXXXXXXX XXXXXXXXXX Captain / Master Relieved And Then Retook Command XXXXXXXXXX XXXXXXXXXX

	1723	*Glasgow*	Sloop				>			>	Philadelphia	[15 Aug 1723] / [22 Aug 1723]	
								South Carolina			[Pennsylvania]	[6 Sept 1723]	
M-H-026	S-G-008												
S-G-008							>	Madeira Island					
Page # 86								[Portugal]					
		5:58,60,82,88 / 8:88,91,96							(Sloop / Glasgow) Captain Taken Prisoner – Mate Took Command / 10 May 1720				

Interact	Ship				Captain / Master		Passage	Arrival / Departure 1		Passage	Arrival / Departure 2		Page
28	Year	Name	Type	Burden	First Name	Last Name	Length	Port	Arrival / Entered Inwards	Length	Port	Arrival / Entered Inwards	86
									Custom In / Entered Out			Custom In / Entered Out	
	MSTR ID#							State / Country	Custom Out / Cleared Out		State / Country	Custom Out / Cleared Out	
	SHIP ID#	Registry Location							Departure			Departure	
	Source							Notes					

	Year / MSTR ID# / SHIP ID# / Source	Name	Type	Burden	First Name	Last Name	Length	Port / State-Country	Arrival dates	Length	Port / State-Country	Arrival dates	
M-W-025 S-U-001 Page # 87 <	1720 M-W-023 S-U-001 6:2	Unity	Sloop		William	Wade	Start	Jamaica		>	Philadelphia Pennsylvania	[20 Dec 1720] XX [31 Jan 1721] XX XXXXXXXXXXXXXX XXXXXXXXXXXXXX	> M-W-025 S-U-001 Page # 87
M-F-008 S-R-010 Page # 87 <	1722 M-P-021 S-R-010 7:79	Richard & Mary	Sloop		Joseph	Parker	Start	Philadelphia [Pennsylvania]	XX [26 Apr 1722] XXX XXXXXXXXXXXXXX [5 Jul 1722]	>	Bristol [England]		
M-S-031 S-U-001 Page # 84 <	1719 – 1720 M-H-026 S-U-001	Unity	Sloop		Miles	Harden / Harding	Start	Philadelphia [Pennsylvania]	XX [22 Dec 1719] XX XXXXXXXXXXXXXX [29 Dec 1719] 18 Jan 1720	>	Suriname		> S-U-001 Page # 87
							>	Philadelphia [Pennsylvania]	[19 May 1720] XX [30 Jun 1720] XX XXXXXXXXXXXXXX XXXXXXXXXXXXXX				M-W-025
	XXXXXXXXXX XXXXXXXXXX Captain / Master Changed Ships XXXXXXXXXX XXXXXXXXXX												
	1721 S-R-010	Richard & Mary	Sloop				Start	Philadelphia [Pennsylvania]	[17 Jan 1721] XX [8 Jun 1721] XXX XXXXXXXXXXXXXX	>	Bristol [England]	Never Left For Port See Next Ship Or Captain	> M-F-008 S-R-010 Page # 87
	XXXXXXXXXX XXXXXXXXXX Captain / Master Changed Ships XXXXXXXXXX XXXXXXXXXX												
M-W-024 S-G-008 Page # 85 <	1721 – 1722 S-G-008	Glasgow	Sloop				Start	Philadelphia [Pennsylvania]	[30 Nov 1721]	>	Sinepuxent [Maryland]		> M-W-024 S-G-008 Page # 85
							>	Philadelphia [Pennsylvania]	[29 Mar 1722]				
	XXXXXXXXXX XXXXXXXXXX Captain / Master Changed Ships XXXXXXXXXX XXXXXXXXXX												
M-S-032 S-U-001 Page # 87 <	1722 S-U-001 5:4,12,53 / 6:10,138 / 7:38,126,138	Unity	Sloop				Start	Virginia		>	Philadelphia [Pennsylvania]	[1 Nov 1722] [29 Nov 1722]	
							>	North Carolina					

Interact	Year	Name	Type	Burden	First Name	Last Name	Length	Port	Arrival/Entered Inwards; Custom In/Entered Out; Custom Out/Cleared Out; Departure	Length	Port	Arrival/Entered Inwards; Custom In/Entered Out; Custom Out/Cleared Out; Departure	Page
28													**87**
M-H-026 / S-R-010 / Page # 86 <	1721 – 1722 / M-F-008 / S-R-010	*Richard & Mary*	Sloop		James	Forster	Start	Philadelphia [Pennsylvania]	XXXXXXXXXXXXXX / XX [17 Jan 1721] XX / [8 Jun 1721]	>	Bristol [England]		> M-P-021 / S-R-010 / Page # 86
							>	Anguilla		>	Philadelphia [Pennsylvania]	[26 Apr 1722] / XXXXXXXXXXXXXX / XX [5 Jul 1722] XX / XXXXXXXXXXXXXX	
	Source: 6:58 / 7:48												
M-H-026 / S-U-001 / Page # 86 <	1720 – 1721 / M-W-025 / S-U-001	*Unity*	Sloop		William	Way	Start	Philadelphia [Pennsylvania]	XX [19 May 1720] XX / [30 Jun 1720] / [28 Jul 1720]	>	Antigua		> M-W-023 / S-U-001 / Page # 86
								XXXXXXXXXX XXXXXXXXXX Captain / Master Relieved And Then Retook Command XXXXXXXXXX XXXXXXXXXX					
M-W-023 / S-U-001 / Page # 86 <							Start	Philadelphia [Pennsylvania]	XX [20 Dec 1720] XX / [31 Jan 1721] / [14 Feb 1721]	>	Virginia		> M-L-001 / S-U-001 / Page # 87
	Source: 5:70,82 / 6:14,18												
M-W-025 / S-U-001 / Page # 87 <	1721 / M-L-011 / S-U-001	*Unity*	Sloop		Hugh	Lowdon	Start	Virginia		>	Philadelphia [Pennsylvania]	8 Jul 1721 / XX [2 Nov 1721] XX / XXXXXXXXXXXXXX / XXXXXXXXXXXXXX	> M-S-032 / S-U-001 / Page # 87
	Source: 6:76												
M-L-011 / S-U-001 / Page # 87 <	1721 / M-S-032 / S-U-001	*Unity*	Sloop		John	Stevenson / Stephenson	Start	Philadelphia [Pennsylvania]	XX [8 Jul 1721] XX / [2 Nov 1721] / [16 Nov 1721]	>	Virginia		> M-H-026 / S-U-001 / Page # 86
							>	Philadelphia [Pennsylvania]	[24 May 1722] / XXXXXXXXXXXXXX / XXXXXXXXXXXXXX / XXXXXXXXXXXXXX	[>]	Virginia		
							XXXXXXXXXX XXXXXXXXXX Captain / Master Changed Ships XXXXXXXXXX XXXXXXXXXX						
M-P-019 / S-H-017 / Page # 83 <	1722 – 1723 / S-H-017	*Henry*	Snow				Start	Philadelphia [Pennsylvania]	XXXXXXXXXXXXXX / XX [11 Oct 1722] XX / [8 Nov 1722]	>	Madeira Island [Portugal]		> M-P-019 / S-H-017 / Page # 83
							[>]	Boston [Massachusetts]	[27 Apr 1723]	>	Philadelphia [Pennsylvania]	[16 May 1723] / XXXXXXXXXXXXXX / XX [27 Jun 1723] XX / XXXXXXXXXXXXXX	
	Source: 6:125,132 / 7:60,130 / 8:54 / 20:91												

YEARS COVERED / 22 Dec 1719 – 7 Jan 1724

Last Name	First Name	MSTR ID#	Page #	19	20	21	22	23	24	Date Range
?										
?	?	M-?-001	1					X		4 Oct 1723
?	?	M-?-002	1		X					27 Dec 1720
?	?	M-?-003	2		X					27 Oct 1720
A										
Abbot	David	M-A-010	56		X	X	X			9 Jun 1720 – 9 Aug 1722
Abbot	John	M-A-009	46					X		27 Jun 1723
Abbot	Robert	M-A-012	80			X				13 Apr 1721 – 7 Dec 1721
"	"	"	"					X		6 Sept 1723 – 17 Oct 1723
Adderly	Abraham	M-A-007	30		X					9 Jun 1720 – 7 Jul 1720
Ainsworth	Thomas	M-A-005	24		X	X				26 May 1720 – 20 Jul 1721
Anderson	Lawrence	M-A-011	61				X			21 Mar 1722 – 12 Apr 1722
Annis	John	M-A-004	20		X	X	X	X		8 Mar 1720 - 11 Oct 1723
Annis Jr	John	M-A-008	40		X					27 Jan 1720
"	"	"	"			X	X	X		27 Jul 1721 – 14 Nov 1723
Annis	William	M-A-001	3				X	X		11 Dec 1722 – 2 May 1723
Argent	William	M-A-013	85		X					3 May 1720
Arthur	Joseph	M-A-002	6		X	X				1 Mar 1720 – 7 Dec 1721
"	"	"	"					X		27 Jun 1723 – 20 Sept 1723
Attwood	Anthony	M-A-006	27		X	X				9 Jun 1720 – 18 May 1721
B										
Bailey	?	M-B-003	2		X					28 Jul 1720
Bailey	Edward	M-B-010	14		X					26 Jul 1720 – 25 Aug 1720
Bailey	James	M-B-029	46			X				24 Aug 1721 – 9 Oct 1721
Ball	John	M-B-013	17			X				10 Aug 1721 - 7 Sept 1721
Barber	John	M-B-026	31			X				30 Mar 1721 – 20 Apr 1721
Barger	Phillip	M-B-020	24		X					21 Jul 1720
Barrington	Richard	M-B-014	19					X		12 Oct 1723 - 29 Nov 1723
Bartlett	John	M-B-001	1				X			8 Oct 1722
Bartlett	John	M-B-002	1					X		16 Mar 1723
Bartlett	John	M-B-038	14		X					23 Jun 1720 – 10 Sept 1720
Bedford	John	M-B-021	25		X	X	X			6 Sept 1720 – 14 Jun 1722
Beeke	Henry	M-B-009	12				X	X		5 Apr 1722 – 6 Jun 1723
Beeke	William	M-B-031	57				X			5 Apr 1722 – 6 Sept 1722
"	"	"	"					X	X	25 Apr 1723 – 16 Jul 1724
Bell	William	M-B-027	32					X		4 Jul 1723
Bennett	Elisha	M-B-006	7			X				5 Jun 1721 – 19 Dec 1721
Bennet	John	M-B-032	66				X			3 Oct 1722 – 8 Nov 1722
"	"	"	"					X		31 Oct 1723 – 17 Dec 1723
Beran	William	M-B-017	22		X					19 May 1720
Bevan	William	M-B-037	82		X					16 Jun 1720 – 23 Jun 1720
Bignell / Bignall / Bicknall	Samuel	M-B-015	19	X	X	X	X			29 Dec 1719 - 23 Nov 1722
Bird	Robert	M-B-033	67					X		16 May 1723 – 29 Jul 1723
Bird	Robert	M-B-035	78					X		17 Dec 1723
Blakey	Charles	M-B-019	23			X	X			30 Mar 1721 – 14 Jun 1722
Bloom	Robert	M-B-011	15					X		25 Jul 1723 – 4 Oct 1723
Bourdet	Samuel	M-B-034	70				X			13 Sept 1722
Boutne / Bourne	Thomas	M-B-023	27				X	X		10 May 1722 – 4 Jul 1723
Brewer	John	M-B-022	26		X					18 Mar 1720 – 19 May 1720
Brown	Bristow	M-B-012	15			X				2 Nov 1721 – 30 Nov 1721
Brown	James	M-B-030	52			X				27 Apr 1721 – 30 Nov 1721

Last Name	First Name	MSTR ID#	Page #	19	20	21	22	23	24	Date Range
B										
Brown	James	M-B-016	22				X	X		15 Nov 1722 – 11 May 1723
Brown	John	M-B-025	29		X					14 Apr 1720
Brown	William	M-B-008	9			X				19 Jun 1721 – 29 Jun 1721
Bull	William	M-B-007	9		X	X	X			11 Jun 1720 – 29 Mar 1722
Burch	Daniel	M-B-024	27					X		4 Jul 1723 – 25 Jul 1723
Burch	David	M-B-036	80		X					8 Jul 1720 – 31 Aug 1720
Burch	John	M-B-028	45				X			12 Apr 1722
Burn	William	M-B-018	23				X			29 Mar 1722 – 3 May 1722
Burrows	Samuel	M-B-005	5				X			16 Aug 1722 – 20 Sept 1720
Butterfield	?	M-B-004	2					X		18 Apr 1723
C										
Car	William	M-C-001	7			X				9 Nov 1721 – 16 Nov 1721
Carpenter	Thomas	M-C-016	75				X			18 Oct 1722 – 1 Nov 1722
"	"	"	"					X		27 Jun 1723
Cassly / Casely	John	M-C-011	42		X					6 Oct 1720 – 28 Nov 1720
"	"	"	"					X		26 Sept 1723 – 21 Oct 1723
Cathoone	James	M-C-006	32			X				28 Sept 1721 – 5 Oct 1721
Cheesman	Thomas	M-C-004	26		X					18 Jun 1729 – 28 Jul 1720
Clarke	John	M-C-003	18		X	X	X	X		27 Jun 1720 - 18 Nov 1723
Clayton	Thomas	M-C-013	51					X		5 Feb 1723 – 4 Apr 1723
Clunn	William	M-C-017	82		X					14 Aug 1720 – 6 Oct 1720
Codd	Robert	M-C-014	55		X	X				27 Dec 1720 – 26 Jun 1721
Collins	Thomas	M-C-002	8				X			23 Aug 1722 – 11 Dec 1722
Combs	Henry	M-C-010	40		X	X				31 Mar 1720 – 25 May 1721
"	"	"	"				X			12 Apr 1722 – 28 Aug 1722
Cooper	Samuel	M-C-008	35		X	X	X			23 Oct 1720 – 3 Dec 1722
Coppel	John	M-C-009	38		X					30 Aug 1720 – 15 Sept 1720
"	"	"	"				X			28 Aug 1722
Cowman	Jeremiah	M-C-007	34					X		26 Feb 1723 – 9 May 1723
Crate	John	M-C-015	61			X				26 Apr 1721
Cropper	Jonathan	M-C-005	28		X					Mar 1720 – 14 Sept 1720
Curtis	Jehu	M-C-012	48	X	X					22 Dec 1719 – 20 Apr 1720
D										
Darrell	John	M-D-006	45			X				23 Jun 1721 – 13 Jul 1721
Davis	Benjamin	M-D-011	53		X	X				16 Jun 1720 – 3 Jan 1721
Davis	James	M-D-009	48			X				8 Jul 1721 – 3 Aug 1721
Davis	William	M-D-010	49		X					28 Apr 1720
De Haes	Barnabas	M-D-012	72		X	X	X			24 Nov 1720 – 19 Jul 1722
"	"	"	"					X		24 Oct 1723 – 21 Nov 1723
De Haes	Johannes	M-D-003	26					X		30 May 1723 – 13 Jun 1723
Dickinson	John	M-D-005	41		X					9 Jan 1720
"	"	"	"		X	X				7 Apr 1720 – 28 Sept 1721
"	"	"	"					X		15 Sept 1723 – 23 Sept 1723
Dickinson	Jonathan	M-D-002	22					X		8 Feb 1723 – 30 May 1723
Dickinson	Joseph	M-D-008	47			X				19 Oct 1721 – 7 Dec 1721
Dobbs	William	M-D-001	13				X			11 Jun 1722 – 15 Oct 1722
Drake	John	M-D-004	28			X				6 Jul 1721 – 27 Jul 1721
Drason	William	M-D-013	81		X	X	X			2 Feb 1722 – 5 Jul 1722
Dunlop	William	M-D-007	46					X		9 May 1723

YEARS COVERED / 22 Dec 1719 – 7 Jan 1724

Last Name	First Name	MSTR ID#	Page #	19	20	21	22	23	24	Date Range
E										
Emmes	Samuel	M-E-002	34				X			18 Oct 1722
Empson	Cornelius	M-E-003	71				X			13 Aug 1722 – 30 Aug 1722
"	"	"	"					X		7 Mar 1723 – 11 Oct 1723
Evans	Joseph	M-E-001	5				X			9 Aug 1722 – 6 Sept 1722
F										
Ferguson	James	M-F-001	50			X				31 Jul 1721 – 7 Sept 1721
Flemming	Thomas	M-F-007	58			X				3 Aug 1721
Forster	James	M-F-008	87			X	X			8 Jun 1721 – 26 Apr 1722
Fox	Samuel	M-F-002	5				X			2 Aug 1722 – 20 Sept 1722
Foy	Edward	M-F-005	24			X	X			23 Nov 1721 – 28 Aug 1722
Fraser	George	M-F-006	36			X				23 Mar 1721 – 8 Jun 1721
Friend	Henry	M-F-003	17		X					26 Jul 1720 - 25 Aug 1720
Fry	Sylvan	M-F-004	23			X				5 Aug 1721 – 2 Nov 1721
G										
Garmston	Paul	M-G-008	28					X		31 Oct 1723 – 5 Dec 1723
Gibbs	John	M-G-005	11			X				7 Aug 1721 – 7 Sept 1721
Gilbert	Ephraim	M-G-002	4	X	X	X				18 Nov 1719 – 11 May 1721
Giffing	Francis	M-G-006	22		X					12 May 1720 – 23 Jun 1720
Glentworth	Thomas	M-G-015	69		X	X	X			14 Jul 1720 – 15 Mar 1722
"	"	"	"					X		18 Apr 1723 – 29 Nov 1723
Gregory	Robert	M-G-012	56		X					19 May 1720
Griffith	Joseph	M-G-011	49		X	X				21 Apr 1720 – 6 Apr 1721
Grigg	George	M-G-017	80				X			29 Mar 1722
Goddard	William	M-G-013	58		X					23 Feb 1720 – 19 May 1720
"	"	"	"		X	X				10 Nov 1720 – 27 Jul 1721
"	"	"	"				X			15 Mar 1722 – 15 Nov 1722
Gordon	Alexander	M-G-014	65		X					25 Jul 1720 – 10 Nov 1720
"	"	"	"			X				20 Apr 1721 – 10 Oct 1721
Gordon	James	M-G-010	38		X					18 Jun 1720 – 14 Jul 1720
"	"	"	"			X	X			3 Apr 1721 – 28 Aug 1722
"	"	"	"					X		10 Jun 1723
Gorham	Joseph	M-G-009	33	X	X					18 Dec 1719 – 28 Mar 1720
"	"	"	"				X	X		16 Apr 1722 – 21 Sept 1723
Gray	Neil	M-G-001	68				X			9 Aug 1722 – 23 Aug 1722
Greenman	Edward	M-G-016	77			X	X	X		19 Dec 1721 – 9 Dec 1723
Griffins	Joseph	M-G-003	68				X			12 Apr 1722 – 17 May 1722
Griffith	William	M-G-007	26					X		11 Oct 1723 – 5 Dec 1723
Gruchy	James	M-G-004	7				X			19 Apr 1722 – 25 Oct 1722
H										
Haddock	Benjamin	M-H-012	29				X			10 Mar 1722 – 15 Nov 1722
Handy	Thomas	M-H-014	30				X			29 Nov 1722 – 11 Dec 1722
Harden / Harding	Aaron	M-H-020	54		X	X	X			7 Mar 1720 – 31 May 1722
Harden / Harding	Miles	M-H-026	86	X	X					29 Dec 1719 – 19 May 1720
"	"	"	"			X	X			17 Jan 1721 – 29 Mar 1722
"	"	"	"				X			1 Nov 1722 – 29 Nov 1722
Hargrave	Charles	M-H-023	70				X	X		10 May 1722 – 4 May 1723
Harvey	Samuel	M-H-007	24		X					26 Aug 1720 – 29 Sept 1720

Last Name	First Name	MSTR ID#	Page #	19	20	21	22	23	24	Date Range
H										
Harris	Benjamin	M-H-011	28				X			27 Feb 1722
Hasell	Joseph	M-H-013	30					X		13 Jun 1723 – 4 Jul 1723
Hawarden	William	M-H-008	27					X	X	9 Dec 1723 – 7 Jan 1724
Hayman	Samuel	M-H-006	16				X			19 Jul 1722
Hill	Crispin	M-H-005	11			X				12 Aug 1721 – 21 Sept 1721
Hillary	Samuel	M-H-025	41				X			12 Jul 1722 – 11 Dec 1722
Hilmont	Lambert	M-H-004	7			X				13 Jul 1721 – 2 Nov 1721
Hodge	John	M-H-019	48		X					6 Aug 1720 – 25 Aug 1720
Holiman	?	M-H-021	55		X					5 Oct 1720
Hollands	Jehoshaphat	M-H-015	31			X	X			9 Nov 1721 – 1 Nov 1722
Hollyman	Samuel	M-H-018	45			X	X			20 Jul 1721 – 19 Jul 1722
Holmes	Robert	M-H-002	4					X		1 Apr 1723 – 13 Jul 1723
Holt	Reeves	M-H-022	69	X						Sept 1719 – 22 Nov 1719
"	"	"	"			X				20 Apr 1721
Holt	Warner	M-H-016	34		X	X	X	X		7 Apr 1720 – 18 Sept 1723
Hopkins	John	M-H-009	27		X					9 Jun 1720 – 28 Jul 1720
Hopkins	John	M-H-010	28				X	X		1 Nov 1722 – 18 Apr 1723
Hopper	Thomas	M-H-024	74				X			24 May 1722 – 14 Jun 1722
Hudson	?	M-H-001	1	X						22 Dec 1719
Hunter	Robert	M-H-003	5				X			18 Oct 1722 – 23 Nov 1722
Hurst	Thomas	M-H-017	35		X					14 Sept 1720 – 13 Dec 1720
Huworth / Howarth	Isaac	M-H-026	82		X					16 Jun 1720 – 10 Nov 1720
J										
Jacobs	Caleb	M-J-006	49		X					14 Mar 1720
Jacobs	Samuel	M-J-007	71		X					15 Sept 1720
"	"	"	"			X	X	X		15 Jun 1721 – 14 Mar 1723
James	Thomas	M-J-002	22					X		15 Aug 1723 – 6 Sept 1723
Jenkins	Matthew	M-J-003	30					X		8 Aug 1723 – 12 Sept 1723
Jenkins	Thomas	M-J-001	2					X		17 Aug 1723
Joel	Thomas	M-J-004	35		X					27 Aug 1720 – 29 Sept 1720
Johnson	Henry	M-J-005	46			X				7 Dec 1721
K										
Keele	William	M-K-001	7				X			26 Apr 1722 – 24 May 1722
Kirle	John	M-K-003	55		X					28 Apr 1720 – 6 Oct 1720
King	George	M-K-002	44	X	X					22 Dec 1719 – 13 May 1720
"	"	"	"		X	X				6 Oct 1720 – 7 Dec 1721
L										
Lambert	George	M-L-001	13					X		13 Jun 1723 – 25 Jul 1723
Lawrence	Lawrence	M-L-009	60					X		2 May 1723 – 22 Aug 1723
Lea / Lee	William	M-L-010	80			X				15 Sept 1721 – 16 Nov 1721
"	"	"	"					X		17 Oct 1723 – 24 Oct 1723
Lindsey	David	M-L-005	25	X	X	X				22 Dec 1719 – 27 Jul 1721
Lindsey	David	M-L-006	30			X				30 May 1721 – 8 Jun 1721
Liston	Robert	M-L-004	23		X					2 Feb 1720 – 7 Mar 1720
Little	Thomas	M-L-008	59					X		9 May 1723 – 20 Sept 1723
Long	Nathaniel	M-L-007	45				X	X		18 Dec 1722 – 24 Dec 1723
Lowdon	Hugh	M-L-011	87			X				8 Jul 1721

YEARS COVERED / 22 Dec 1719 – 7 Jan 1724

L

Last Name	First Name	MSTR ID#	Page #	19	20	21	22	23	24	Date Range
Lowtor	Thomas	M-L-002	15				X			17 Dec 1723 – 24 Dec 1723
Lusher	Joseph	M-L-012	85			X	X	X		5 Oct 1721 – 8 Aug 1723
Lynn	Charles	M-L-003	21		X					2 Feb 1720

M

Last Name	First Name	MSTR ID#	Page #	19	20	21	22	23	24	Date Range
Mackey	John	M-M-007	14				X	X		25 Oct 1722 – 14 Nov 1723
Manners	John	M-M-008	15			X				14 Jul 1721 – 7 Sept 1721
Manning	William	M-M-015	82					X		26 Sept 1723
Mariner	Nathaniel	M-M-006	9			X				10 Aug 1721 – 7 Sept 1721
Martindal	Isaac	M-M-004	8					X		22 Aug 1723 – 12 Sept 1723
Maugier	Edward	M-M-005	8		X					7 Jul 1720
Mayberry / Maybury	William	M-M-002	6					X		6 Jun 1723 – 5 Dec 1723
Meredith	Owen	M-M-013	75		X					7 Apr 1720 – 23 Jun 1720
"	"	"	"			X	X			18 May 1721 – 6 Sept 1722
Moale	Samuel	M-M-010	39		X					4 Jan 1720 – 18 Jan 1720
"	"	"	"		X					19 May 1720 – 23 Jun 1720
Montague	Thomas	M-M-012	61		X					14 Jul 1720
Moore	Peter	M-M-009	30	X	X					29 Dec 1719 – 18 Jan 1720
Moorecraft	John	M-M-003	80		X					20 Oct 1720 – 27 Oct 1720
Morris	Isaac	M-M-011	57				X	X		15 Nov 1722 – 18 Apr 1723
Munford	Thomas	M-M-014	78					X		28 Nov 1723
Murgatroyd	James	M-M-001	6			X				9 Nov 1721 – 7 Dec 1721

N

Last Name	First Name	MSTR ID#	Page #	19	20	21	22	23	24	Date Range
Naylor	Samuel	M-N-006	81	X	X					22 Dec 1719 – 29 Sept 1720
"	"	"	"					X		5 Dec 1723
New	Thomas	M-N-002	11					X		13 Jun 1723 – 4 Jul 1723
Newcomb	Richard	M-N-001	4		X					11 May 1720
Nisbet	Joseph	M-N-005	70			X				12 Apr 1721 – 27 Apr 1721
Northey	Samuel	M-N-003	31		X					28 Nov 1720 – 27 Dec 1720
Norwood	Henry	M-N-004	62				X	X	X	18 Dec 1722 – 16 Jul 1724

O

Last Name	First Name	MSTR ID#	Page #	19	20	21	22	23	24	Date Range
Oliver	John	M-O-001	42			X	X			3 Aug 1721 – 29 Nov 1722
Owen	John	M-O-003	51	X	X	X	X	X		29 Dec 1719 – 9 May 1723
Owen	Nathaniel	M-O-002	43	X	X					6 Dec 1719 – 28 Apr 1720
"	"	"	"		X					24 Nov 1720 – 27 Dec 1720
"	"	"	"			X	X			7 Aug 1721 – 15 Nov 1722

P

Last Name	First Name	MSTR ID#	Page #	19	20	21	22	23	24	Date Range
Palmer	Joseph	M-P-003	16		X					19 May 1720 – 31 Jul 1720
Palmer	Robert	M-P-010	37	X	X	X				22 Dec 1719 – 2 Mar 1721
"	"	"	"				X			5 Apr 1722 – 14 Jun 1722
"	"	"	"					X		11 Oct 1723 – 29 Nov 1723
Parham	Thomas	M-P-008	33		X					12 May 1720 – 19 May 1720
Parker	John	M-P-019	83		X	X	X	X		27 Apr 1720 – 13 Oct 1723

P

Last Name	First Name	MSTR ID#	Page #	19	20	21	22	23	24	Date Range
Parker	Joseph	M-P-020	84		X					7 Apr 1720 – 18 Aug 1720
"	"	"	"			X				16 Mar 1721 – 13 Apr 1721
"	"	"	"			X				28 Aug 1721 – 5 Oct 1721
Parker	Joseph	M-P-021	86				X			5 Jul 1722
Parker	Samuel	M-P-012	48				X			16 Aug 1722 – 18 Oct 1722
Pattison	William	M-P-007	30					X		25 Jul 1723 – 29 Jul 1723
Pearce	Laborious	M-P-014	60					X		26 Sept 1723
Peartree	James	M-P-017	74	X						22 Nov 1719
"	"	"	"		X	X	X			28 Jul 1720 – 10 May 1722
"	"	"	"					X		13 Apr 1723 – 24 Aug 1723
Peel	Anthony	M-P-016	66	X	X	X	X	X		22 Dec 1719 – 24 Dec 1723
Peer	William	M-P-009	36		X					20 Apr 1720 – 16 Jun 1720
Peters	Peter	M-P-006	21		X	X				30 Jun 1720 – 27 Apr 1721
Peters	Peter	M-P-005	19				X			5 Jul 1722
Petty	Thomas	M-P-015	65			X				1 Aug 1721 – 24 Aug 1721
Phillips	Jacob	M-P-001	2					X		4 May 1723 – 11 May 1723
Phillips	Matthew	M-P-011	44	X	X					22 Dec 1719 – 3 Nov 1720
"	"	"	"		X					24 Nov 1720
Phillips	Matthew	M-P-018	77				X	X		8 Nov 1722 – 7 Nov 1723
Phipps	John	M-P-004	17		X					8 Oct 1720 – 27 Oct 1720
Price	John	M-P-002	8				X			26 Apr 1722 – 3 May 1722
Prichard	Joseph	M-P-013	59		X	X	X	X		7 Mar 1720 – 24 Oct 1723

R

Last Name	First Name	MSTR ID#	Page #	19	20	21	22	23	24	Date Range
Radford	Bartholomew	M-R-001	2	X	X					22 Dec 1719 – 26 Jun 1720
Randal	Thomas	M-R-004	14			X	X			13 Feb 1721 – 30 Jul 1722
Read	John	M-R-012	55		X	X	X			3 Nov 1720 – 18 Dec 1722
Read	John	M-R-006	22					X		24 Dec 1723
Read	Thomas	M-R-017	73		X	X				3 Jun 1720 – 9 Mar 1721
"	"	"	"			X				27 Jul 1721 – 16 Nov 1721
Reeve	John	M-R-011	53				X	X		14 Jun 1722 – 5 Dec 1722
Rice	John	M-R-015	67		X					17 Nov 1720
Richards	John	M-R-002	7					X		9 Dec 1723
Richards	John	M-R-008	29		X	X	X	X		18 Sept 1720 – 4 Oct 1723
Richmond	John	M-R-014	63		X					5 May 1720 – 1 Jun 1720
"	"	"	"		X	X	X			24 Nov 1720 – 18 Dec 1722
"	"	"	"					X		24 Oct 1723 – 17 Dec 1723
Rime / Rimes	William	M-R-005	17			X				2 May 1721 - 29 Jun 1721
Rivers	Shadlock	M-R-016	67	X	X	X	X	X		22 Dec 1719 2 May 1723
Roach	Nicholas	M-R-007	28		X					5 May 1720 – 8 Oct 1720
Roe	Parker	M-R-009	32			X				9 Nov 1721 – 30 Nov 1721
Royal	Joseph	M-R-013	58		X					6 Jun 1720
Ruddock	Joseph	M-R-003	13					X		12 Sept 1723 – 31 Oct 1723
Rush	William	M-R-010	37			X	X			10 Aug 1721 – 29 Mar 1722
"	"	"	"					X		4 May 1723

YEARS COVERED / 22 Dec 1719 – 7 Jan 1724

S

Last Name	First Name	MSTR ID#	Page #	19	20	21	22	23	24	Date Range
Saltus	Francis	M-S-009	20		X					8 Aug 1720 - 25 Aug 1720
"	"	"	"				X			12 Apr 1722- 17 May 1722
Scott	John	M-S-026	50		X	X				6 Dec 1720 – 21 Sept 1721
"	"	"	"					X		11 Jul 1723
Searle	John	M-S-028	65		X					18 Aug 1720 – 17 Oct 1720
Seavy	Stephen	M-S-011	21			X				29 May 1721 – 13 Jul 1721
Sharp	Asser	M-S-021	47		X					13 Aug 1720 – 15 Sept 1720
Simmons	Stephen	M-S-027	61	X	X					22 Dec 1719 – 31 Mar 1720
"	"	"	"			X	X			18 May 1721 – 6 Feb 1722
"	"	"	"				X			21 Mar 1722 – 11 Dec 1722
Sims	Richard	M-S-006	12		X					28 Apr 1720 – 29 Sept 1720
Sipkins	?	M-S-005	8		X					10 Nov 1720
Slyfield	George	M-S-030	78				X	X		21 Jun 1722 – 14 Nov 1723
Smith	Christopher	M-S-016	29		X					24 Oct 1720 – 24 Nov 1720
Smith	Edward	M-S-004	3			X				24 Jun 1721 – 4 Oct 1721
Smith	Joseph	M-S-001	3		X					7 Mar 1720 – 27 Dec 1720
"	"	"	"				X			26 Apr 1722
"	"	"	"				X			7 Jun 1722 - 10 Oct 1722
Spafford	William	M-S-019	39		X					1 Jun 1720 – 7 Oct 1720
"	"	"	"			X	X	X		27 Apr 1721 – 21 Nov 1723
Sparks	Edward	M-S-015	29		X					26 May 1720 – 20 Dec 1720
Spofforth	Samuel	M-S-022	47			X				12 Apr 1721 – 7 Sept 1721
Spofforth	Robert	M-S-023	47				X			19 Apr 1722 – 17 May 1722
Stammers	John	M-S-008	13		X					20 Apr 1720 – 12 May 1720
Stevens	Henry	M-S-031	84	X	X	X				22 Dec 1719 – 17 Aug 1721
Stevens	Richard	M-S-007	12		X					19 May 1720 – 27 Aug 1720
Stockin / Stocken	John	M-S-032	87			X	X	X		2 Nov 1721 – 16 May 1723
Stockin / Stocken	Thomas	M-S-029	76		X	X				15 Jul 1720 – 30 Nov 1721
"	"	"	"				X	X		3 Oct 1722 – 6 Sept 1723
Story	Samuel	M-S-002	3		X					14 Jul 1720 – 4 Aug 1720
Stout	John	M-S-012	21				X			26 Apr 1722 - 31 May 1722
Straiton / Straton	James	M-S-013	23				X			14 Jun 1722 – 19 Jul 1722
Styles	Edward	M-S-017	35		X					15 Sept 1720 – 13 Oct 1720
Styles	John	M-S-025	49		X					5 May 1720 – 24 Oct 1720
Sutton	Edward	M-S-024	48		X					7 Jul 1720
Swain	Jonathan	M-S-020	42				X			22 Jul 1722
"	"	"	"						X	1724
Swain	William	M-S-014	26				X			16 Aug 1722 – 27 Sept 1722
Sylvan	Nicholas	M-S-018	36			X				Jun 1721 – 23 Nov 1721

T

Last Name	First Name	MSTR ID#	Page #	19	20	21	22	23	24	Date Range
Taylor	Henry	M-T-010	64		X	X	X	X		14 Jul 1720 – 21 Nov 1723
Terrell	Thomas	M-T-011	65		X					19 Jul 1720 – 10 Nov 1720
Thomas	Joshua	M-T-008	32			X				15 Jun 1721 – 29 Jun 1721
Thornton	John	M-T-007	31			X	X			26 Oct 1721 – 10 Mar 1722
Thorp	?	M-T-001	1	X	X					22 Nov 1719 – 19 May 1720
Toest	Joseph	M-T-002	6			X				1 Aug 1721
Townsend	Robert	M-T-003	9					X		25 Apr 1723 – 9 May 1723
Tucker	Benjamin	M-T-009	36				X			26 Apr 1722 – 31 May 1722
Tucker	John	M-T-004	9				X			12 Apr 1722 – 7 Jun 1722
Tudor	Thomas	M-T-006	17		X					5 Oct 1720 - 20 Oct 1720
Turner	Joseph	M-T-012	79					X		14 Jan 1723 – 30 May 1723
Tynes	David	M-T-005	11		X					11 Aug 1720 – 8 Sept 1720

V

Last Name	First Name	MSTR ID#	Page #	19	20	21	22	23	24	Date Range
Vance	James	M-V-002	20		X					14 Mar 1720
Vesey	John	M-V-004	32			X				7 Sept 1721 – 28 Sept 1721
Vinning	Abraham	M-V-003	25		X	X	X	X		7 Mar 1720 – 8 Aug 1723
Virr	Henry	M-V-001	16		X	X	X			13 Nov 1720 – 29 Mar 1722
Vokes	Bartholomew	M-V-005	82				X			23 Mar 1722 – 6 Sept 1722

W

Last Name	First Name	MSTR ID#	Page #	19	20	21	22	23	24	Date Range
Wade	William	M-W-023	86		X					20 Dec 1720
Wair / Wiar	Elias	M-W-011	10		X	X	X	X		1 Jun 1720 – 7 Sept 1723
Wallace	William	M-W-022	79		X	X				13 Oct 1720 – 16 Nov 1721
"	"	"	"				X	X		18 Dec 1722 – 14 Mar 1723
Warden	William	M-W-024	85		X					10 May 1720 – 11 Aug 1720
"	"	"	"					X		15 Aug 1723 – 6 Sept 1723
Watson	Matthew	M-W-020	73	X						29 Dec 1719
Way	William	M-W-025	87		X					30 Jun 1720 – 28 Jul 1720
"	"	"	"			X				31 Jan 1721 – 14 Feb 1721
Webb	Nicholas	M-W-017	52	X	X					9 Dec 1719 – 1 Dec 1720
Weldon	Mark	M-W-019	54				X			5 Jul 1722
Wellman / Willman	Jehoshaphat / Joseph	M-W-007	16				X	X		10 May 1722 – 9 May 1723
Wells	Francis	M-W-006	15		X	X	X			31 Mar 1720 – 19 Apr 1722
Wells	Henry	M-W-005	13					X	X	25 Jul 1723 – 7 Jan 1724
West	Joseph	M-W-015	50			X				14 Sept 1721
Wester	Thomas	M-W-003	11			X				9 Nov 1721
White	Henry	M-W-009	19		X					9 Jun 1720 - 21 Jul 1720
Whither	William	M-W-014	43			X				25 May 1721 – 29 Jun 1721
"	"	"	"				X	X		16 Aug 1722 – 21 Nov 1723
Whitney	David	M-W-013	32				X			9 Aug 1722 – 6 Sept 1722
Wilkins	James	M-W-018	53			X	X			2 Mar 1721 – 14 Jun 1722
"	"	"	"					X		21 Nov 1723
Wilkinson	George	M-W-004	12		X					1 Dec 1720 – 13 Dec 1720
Williams	John	M-W-012	31			X				18 May 1721 – 21 Jun 1721
Willocks	James	M-W-010	21					X		14 Nov 1723 - 24 Dec 1723
Wilson	Garshom	M-W-016	50					X		29 Aug 1723 – 12 Sept 1723
Wilson	Matthew	M-W-001	4		X					31 Mar 1720 – 14 Apr 1720
Wood	John	M-W-008	17					X		26 Sept 1723
Wooton / Wooten	Matthew	M-W-021	73		X					9 Jun 1720 – 17 Nov 1720
Wright	Thomas	M-W-002	11		X					26 Jul 1720 – 1 Sept 1720

YEARS COVERED / 22 Dec 1719 – 7 Jan 1724

?

Ship Names	Type	Ship ID#	Page #	19	20	21	22	23	24	Date Range
?	Sloop	S-?-001	1					X		4 Oct 1723
?	?	S-?-002	1				X			8 Oct 1722
?	?	S-?-003	1					X		16 Mar 1723
?	?	S-?-004	1	X						22 Dec 1719
?	Schooner	S-?-005	1	X	X					22 Nov 1719 – 19 May 1720
?	?	S-?-006	1		X					27 Dec 1720
?	Sloop	S-?-007	2	X	X					22 Dec 1719 – 26 Jun 1720
?	?	S-?-008	2					X		17 Aug 1723
?	?	S-?-009	2					X		4 May 1723 – 11 May 1723
?	Brigantine	S-?-010	2		X					28 Jul 1720
?	?	S-?-011	2					X		18 Apr 1723
?	Brigantine	S-?-012	2		X					27 Oct 1720
?	?	S-?-013	37					X		4 May 1723
?	Sloop	S-?-014	42				X			22 Jul 1722
?	Sloop	S-?-015	44	X	X					22 Dec 1719 – 13 May 1720
?	Sloop	S-?-016	65		X					19 Jul 1720
?	?	S-?-017	69	X						Sept 1719 – 22 Nov 1719
?	?	S-?-018	74					X		13 Apr 1723 – 24 Aug 1723

A

Ship Names	Type	Ship ID#	Page #	19	20	21	22	23	24	Date Range
Abigail	Brigantine	S-A-012	82		X					14 Aug 1720 – 10 Nov 1720
Abigail	Brigantine	S-A-011	41				X			12 Jul 1722
Adventure	Sloop	S-A-001	3		X					7 Mar 1720 – 27 Dec 1720
Adventure	Brigantine	S-A-002	3				X	X		11 Dec 1722 – 2 May 1723
Adventure	Sloop	S-A-003	50			X				31 Jul 1721
Adventure	Sloop	S-A-013	85			X				5 Oct 1721 – 24 Oct 1721
Ann	Sloop	S-A-013	82,84		X	X				16 Jun 1720 – 17 Aug 1721
Anne	Sloop	S-A-004	3		X					14 Jul 1720 – 4 Aug 1720
Anne	Sloop	S-A-005	3				X			26 Apr 1722
Anne	Brigantine	S-A-006	3			X				24 Jun 1721 – 4 Oct 1721
Anne	Sloop	S-A-007	4					X		1 Apr 1723 – 13 Jul 1723
Anne	Sloop	S-A-008	66,67,68				X			5 Apr 1722 – 23 Aug 1722
Antelope	Sloop	S-A-010	70,71			X	X			15 Jun 1721 – 13 Sept 1722
Arcadia	Sloop	S-A-009	56		X	X	X			19 May 1720 – 9 Aug 1722

B

Ship Names	Type	Ship ID#	Page #	19	20	21	22	23	24	Date Range
Bachelor	Sloop	S-B-001	4		X					31 Mar 1720 – 14 Apr 1720
Bedminster	Ship	S-B-013	38		X					18 Jun 1720 – 14 Jul 1720
Beginning	Sloop	S-B-016	58		X	X	X			6 Jun 1720 – 15 Nov 1722
Benjamin	Sloop	S-B-002	4	X	X	X				18 Nov 1719 – 11 May 1721
Benjamin	Schooner	S-B-003	4		X					11 May 1720
Benjamin	Sloop	S-B-004	5				X			16 Aug 1722 – 20 Sept 1720
Benjamin	Brigantine	S-B-005	5			X				20 Jul 1721 – 23 Nov 1721
Benjamin & Mary	Sloop	S-B-006	5				X			18 Oct 1722 – 23 Nov 1722
Bersheba	Sloop	S-B-007	5				X			2 Aug 1722 – 20 Sept 1722
Betty	Sloop	S-B-008	66,68	X	X	X	X			22 Dec 1719 –17 May 1722
Betty	Ship	S-B-018	63		X	X	X			24 Nov 1720 – 18 Dec 1722
Blessing	Sloop	S-B-009	5				X			9 Aug 1722 – 6 Sept 1722
Bon-Adventure	Snow	S-B-021	81	X	X					22 Dec 1719 – 29 Sept 1720
Bon-Adventure	Sloop	S-B-014	50			X				24 Aug 1721 – 14 Sept 1721
Boneta	Brigantine	S-B-010	5			X				9 Nov 1721 – 7 Dec 1721
Boneta	Sloop	S-B-020	70				X			8 Oct 1722 – 25 Oct 1722
Bonneville	Sloop	S-B-019	69					X		18 Apr 1723 – 29 Nov 1723
Bristol	Brigantine	S-B-017	59					X		9 May 1723 – 24 Oct 1723
Britannia	Snow	S-B-015	55		X	X	X			5 Oct 1720- 18 Dec 1722
Britannia	Brigantine	S-B-011	6					X		6 Jun 1723 – 5 Dec 1723
Builders Adventure	Sloop	S-B-012	6			X				1 Aug 1721

C

Ship Names	Type	Ship ID#	Page #	19	20	21	22	23	24	Date Range
Caesar	Brigantine	S-C-017	80,81		X	X	X	X		8 Jul 1720 – 5 Dec 1723
Carolina Packet	Ship	S-C-011	37					X		11 Oct 1723 – 29 Nov 1723
Carpenter	Sloop	S-C-016	80,81,83			X	X			13 Apr 1721 – 5 Jul 1722
Carpenter	Sloop	S-C-015	76,79					X		14 Mar 1723 – 6 Sept 1723
Catherine	Ship	S-C-002	7			X				9 Nov 1721 – 16 Nov 1721
Charles	Sloop	S-C-003	6		X	X				1 Mar 1720 – 7 Dec 1721
Charles	Sloop	S-C-012	40				X			12 Apr 1722 – 28 Aug 1722
Charming Sally	Ship	S-C-004	7				X			19 Apr 1722 – 25 Oct 1722
Charming Molly	Ship	S-C-005	7					X		9 Dec 1723
Clarendon Packet	Sloop	S-C-006	7			X				5 Jun 1721 – 19 Dec 1721
Clementine	Brigantine	S-C-007	6					X		27 Jun 1723 – 20 Sept 1723
Clemmel	Sloop	S-C-014	43		X					24 Nov 1720 – 27 Dec 1720
Cocoa Nut	Sloop	S-C-008	7			X				13 Jul 1721 – 2 Nov 1721
Concord	Sloop	S-C-013	41		X					9 Jan 1720
Content	Sloop	S-C-009	7				X			26 Apr 1722 – 24 May 1722
Cutwater	Sloop	S-C-010	8				X			26 Apr 1722 – 3 May 1722

D

Ship Names	Type	Ship ID#	Page #	19	20	21	22	23	24	Date Range
Deborah	Sloop	S-D-001	8		X					10 Nov 1720
Deborah	Sloop	S-D-009	41		X	X				7 Apr 1720 – 28 Sept 1721
"	"	"	"					X		15 Sept 1723 – 23 Sept 1723
Digby	Sloop	S-D-002	8				X			23 Aug 1722 – 11 Dec 1722
Diligence	Sloop	S-D-012	74	X						22 Nov 1719
Dolphin	Sloop	S-D-008	37	X	X	X				22 Dec 1719 – 2 Mar 1721
Dolphin	Sloop	S-D-004	8		X					7 Jul 1720
Dolphin	Sloop	S-D-007	37			X	X			10 Aug 1721 – 29 Mar 1722
Dolphin	Sloop	S-D-003	8					X		22 Aug 1723 – 12 Sept 1723
Dolphin	Sloop	S-D-011	63,64		X	X	X	X		5 May 1720 – 21 Nov 1723
Dorothy	Ship	S-D-005	9		X	X	X			11 Jun 1720 – 29 Mar 1722
Dove	Brigantine	S-D-010	61,62		X	X	X	X	X	14 Jul 1720 – 16 Jul 1724
Duck	Sloop	S-D-006	9					X		25 Apr 1723 – 9 May 1723

E

Ship Names	Type	Ship ID#	Page #	19	20	21	22	23	24	Date Range
Elizabeth	Sloop	S-E-001	9			X				19 Jun 1721 – 29 Jun 1721
Elizabeth	Sloop	S-E-002	9			X				10 Aug 1721 – 7 Sept 1721
Elizabeth	Sloop	S-E-008	38					X		10 Jun 1723
Elizabeth & Anne	Sloop	S-E-003	9				X			12 Apr 1722 – 7 Jun 1722
Elizabeth & Hannah	Sloop	S-E-007	10		X	X	X	X		1 Jun 1720 – 7 Sept 1723
Elizabeth & Martha	Sloop	S-E-004	11			X				7 Aug 1721 – 7 Sept 1721

YEARS COVERED / 22 Dec 1719 – 7 Jan 1724

Ship Names	Type	Ship ID#	Page #	19	20	21	22	23	24	Date Range
E										
Endeavor	Sloop	S-E-005	11		X					26 Jul 1720 – 1 Sept 1720
Endeavor	Sloop	S-E-010	65,66		X	X	X			25 Jul 1720 – 8 Nov 1722
Endeavor	Sloop	S-E-011	70				X	X		11 Dec 1722 – 4 May 1723
Endeavor	Sloop	S-E-012	79		X	X				13 Oct 1720 – 16 Nov 1721
"	"	"	"				X	X		18 Dec 1722 – 30 May 1723
Endeavor	Brigantine	S-E-013	41				X			11 Dec 1722
Esther	Brigantine	S-E-009	46					X		9 May 1723 - 27 Jun 1723
Exchange	Sloop	S-E-006	11		X					11 Aug 1720 – 8 Sept 1720
F										
Faro	Sloop	S-F-001	11					X		13 Jun 1723 – 4 Jul 1723
Fancy	Sloop	S-F-002	11			X				12 Aug 1721 – 21 Sept 1721
Fancy	Sloop	S-F-003	11			X				9 Nov 1721
Fazackerly	Sloop	S-F-004	12		X					1 Dec 1720 – 13 Dec 1720
Fisher	Sloop	S-F-005	12		X					28 Apr 1720 – 29 Sept 1720
Fortune	Ship	S-F-006	12		X					19 May 1720 – 27 Aug 1720
Four Brothers	Sloop	S-F-007	12				X			5 Apr 1722 – 6 Jun 1723
Francis & Elizabeth	Sloop	S-F-008	13		X					20 Apr 1720 – 12 May 1720
Francis & Mary	Sloop	S-F-011	50		X	X				6 Dec 1720 – 21 Sept 1721
"	"	"	"					X		11 Jul 1723 – 12 Sept 1723
Free Gift	Sloop	S-F-009	13				X			11 Jun 1722 – 15 Oct 1722
Friendship	Sloop	S-F-010	13					X		13 Jun 1723 – 25 Jul 1723
G										
Gambole	Ship	S-G-001	13					X		12 Sept 1723 – 31 Oct 1723
George	Sloop	S-G-007	45			X	X			23 Jun 1721 – 12 Apr 1722
George	Ship	S-G-002	13					X	X	25 Jul 1723 – 7 Jan 1724
Glascow	Sloop	S-G-008	85,86		X					3 May 1720
"	"	"	"		X					10 May 1720 – 11 Aug 1720
"	"	"	"			X	X			30 Nov 1721 – 29 Mar 1722
"	"	"	"					X		15 Aug 1723 – 6 Sept 1723
Globe	Ship	S-G-003	14				X	X		25 Oct 1722 – 14 Nov 1723
Grace & Elizabeth	Sloop	S-G-006	42			X	X			3 Nov 1721 – 29 Nov 1722
Greyhound	Sloop	S-G-004	14		X					26 Jul 1720 – 25 Aug 1720
Greyhound	Ship	S-G-005	38				X			28 Aug 1722
H										
Hamstead	Sloop	S-H-001	14			X	X			13 Feb 1721 – 30 Jul 1722
Hamstead Galley	Ship	S-H-002	15		X	X	X			31 Mar 1720 – 19 Apr 1722
Hannah	Ship	S-H-010	40		X					27 Jan 1720
Hannah	Sloop	S-H-009	40		X	X				31 Mar 1720 – 25 May 1721
Hannah	Sloop	S-H-003	15					X		17 Dec 1723 – 24 Dec 1723
Hannah	Brigantine	S-H-012	49		X	X				14 Mar 1720 – 6 Apr 1721
Hanover	Ship	S-H-013	51	X	X	X	X	X		29 Dec 1719 – 4 Apr 1723
Hastings	Sloop	S-H-014	65,67		X					10 Nov 1720 – 17 Nov 1720
Hawk	Sloop	S-H-004	15					X		25 Jul 1723 – 4 Oct 1723
Henry	Sloop	S-H-005	15			X				2 Nov 1721 – 30 Nov 1721
Henry	Sloop	S-H-006	15			X				14 Jul 1721 – 7 Sept 1721
Henry	Snow	S-H-017	83				X	X		11 Oct 1722 – 13 Oct 1723
Hope	Sloop	S-H-007	16				X	X		10 May 1722 – 9 May 1723

Ship Names	Type	Ship ID#	Page #	19	20	21	22	23	24	Date Range
H										
Hope	Brigantine	S-H-015	71,72					X		7 Mar 1723 – 21 Nov 1723
Hopeful Betty	Sloop	S-H-016	77				X	X		29 Nov 1722 – 9 Dec 1723
Hopewell	Sloop	S-H-018	14		X					23 Jun 1720 – 10 Sept 1720
Hoy Delaware	?	S-H-008	16				X			19 Jul 1722
Hudson Galley	Ship	S-H-011	45			X	X	X		20 Jul 1721 – 24 Dec 1723
I										
Illustrious	Ship	S-I-001	16		X	X	X			13 Nov 1720 – 29 Mar 1722
Industry	Sloop	S-I-002	16		X					19 May 1720 – 31 Jul 1720
Isaac & Mary	Sloop	S-I-003	69			X				20 Apr 1721 – 11 May 1721
J										
James & Mary	Ship	S-J-001	17			X				10 Aug 1721 - 7 Sept 1721
Jane	Brigantine	S-J-002	17			X				2 May 1721 - 29 Jun 1721
Jane	Sloop	S-J-003	17		X					8 Oct 1720 - 27 Oct 1720
Jane	Sloop	S-J-011	44		X					24 Nov 1720
Jane	Sloop	S-J-010	43			X				25 May 1721 – 29 Jun 1721
Jenny	Ship	S-J-004	17		X					5 Oct 1720 - 20 Oct 1720
Jeremiah	Scallop	S-J-005	17					X		26 Sept 1723
John	Sloop	S-J-006	17		X					26 Jul 1720 - 25 Aug 1720
John & Mary	Sloop	S-J-007	18		X	X	X	X		27 Jun 1720 – 18 Nov 1723
John & Sarah	Sloop	S-J-014	73,74	X	X	X				29 Dec 1719 – 25 May 1721
John& Thomas	Sloop	S-J-008	19		X					9 Jun 1720 – 21 Jul 1720
Joseph	Ship	S-J-012	66					X		31 Oct 1723 – 17 Dec 1723
Joseph & John	Brigantine	S-J-009	19				X			5 Jul 1722
Judith	Sloop	S-J-013	70			X				20 Apr 1721 – 27 Apr 1721
K										
Kings Fisher	Schooner	S-K-001	19					X		12 Oct 1723 - 29 Nov 1723
L										
Laurel	Ship	S-L-006	38		X					30 Aug 1720 – 15 Sept 1720
Lincoln-shire	Sloop	S-L-009	74,77,78			X	X	X		8 Jun 1721 – 17 Dec 1723
Little Anne	Sloop	S-L-001	19	X	X	X	X			29 Dec 1719 - 23 Nov 1722
Little Betty	Sloop	S-L-008	73		X					13 Oct 1720 – 17 Nov 1720
Lennox Galley	Sloop	S-L-007	69,70,71			X	X	X		18 May 1721 – 14 Mar 1723
Lennox Galley	Ship	S-L-002	20		X					14 Mar 1720
London Hope	Ship	S-L-003	20		X	X	X	X		8 Mar 1720 – 11 Oct 1723
Love	Sloop	S-L-004	20		X					8 Aug 1720 - 25 Aug 1720
"	"	"					X			12 Apr 1722- 17 May 1722
Loyal Burnett	Sloop	S-L-010	75,76,77			X	X	X		18 May 1721 – 27 Jun 1723
Lydia	Sloop	S-L-005	21		X	X				30 Jun 1720 - 27 Apr 1721

YEARS COVERED / 22 Dec 1719 – 7 Jan 1724

M

Ship Names	Type	Ship ID#	Page #	19	20	21	22	23	24	Date Range
MacCollum	Ship	S-M-001	21		X					2 Feb 1720
Margaret	Sloop	S-M-027	55		X	X				28 Apr 1720 – 26 Jun 1721
Margaret	Sloop	S-M-002	3				X			7 Jun 1722 - 10 Oct 1722
Margaret	Sloop	S-M-030	73		X	X				3 Jun 1720 – 9 Mar 1721
Martha & Elizabeth	Ship	S-M-003	21					X		14 Nov 1723 - 24 Dec 1723
Martha & Mary	Schooner	S-M-026	53		X	X	X	X		16 Jun 1720 – 5 Dec 1723
Mary	Brigantine	S-M-004	21			X				29 May 1721 - 13 Jul 1721
Mary	Sloop	S-M-005	21				X			26 Apr 1722 - 31 May 1722
Mary	Sloop	S-M-006	22				X	X		15 Nov 1722 – 11 May 1723
Mary	Sloop	S-M-007	22					X		24 Dec 1723
Mary	Sloop	S-M-008	22					X		8 Feb 1723 – 30 May 1723
Mary	Sloop	S-M-009	22		X					12 May 1720 – 23 Jun 1720
Mary	Ship	S-M-010	22		X					19 May 1720
Mary	Sloop	S-M-011	22					X		15 Aug 1723 – 6 Sept 1723
Mary	Ship	S-M-012	23				X			14 Jun 1722 – 19 Jul 1722
Mary	Ship	S-M-031	82,83		X					27 Apr 1720 – 23 Jun 1720
Mary	Sloop	S-M-025	43	X	X					6 Dec 1719 – 28 Apr 1720
Mary	Sloop	S-M-029	70,71		X	X				15 Sept 1720 – 27 Apr 1721
Mary & Anne	Sloop	S-M-013	23				X			29 Mar 1722 – 3 May 1722
Mary & Catherine	Brigantine	S-M-014	23			X				5 Aug 1721 – 2 Nov 1721
Mary Galley	Ship	S-M-028	61	X	X					22 Dec 1719 – 31 Mar 1720
Mary Galley	Ship	S-M-015	23		X					2 Feb 1720 – 7 Mar 1720
Mary Hope	Sloop	S-M-022	42		X					6 Oct 1720 – 28 Nov 1720
Mary Hope	Sloop	S-M-024	42			X				3 Aug 1721 – 19 Oct 1721
Mary Hope	Scallop	S-M-023	42					X		26 Sept 1723 – 21 Oct 1723
Mayflower	Schooner	S-M-016	23			X	X			30 Mar 1721 – 14 Jun 1722
Mayflower	Sloop	S-M-017	24		X	X				26 May 1720 – 20 Jul 1721
Mayflower	Schooner	S-M-018	24		X					21 Jul 1720
Milford Galley	Ship	S-M-019	24			X	X			23 Nov 1721 – 28 Aug 1722
Modena	Sloop	S-M-020	24		X					26 Aug 1720 – 29 Sept 1720
Montrose	Brigantine	S-M-021	25	X	X	X				22 Dec 1719 – 27 Jul 1721

N

Ship Names	Type	Ship ID#	Page #	19	20	21	22	23	24	Date Range
Nancy	Snow	S-N-001	25		X	X	X			6 Sept 1720 – 14 Jun 1722
Neptune	Ship	S-N-002	25		X	X	X	X		7 Mar 1720 – 8 Aug 1723
Neptune	Sloop	S-N-003	26		X					16 Jun 1720 – 28 Jul 1720
Neptune	Sloop	S-N-004	26				X			16 Aug 1722 – 27 Sept 1722
Neptune	Brigantine	S-N-009	59					X		30 May 1723- 20 Sept 1723
Newport	Sloop	S-N-005	26		X					18 Mar 1720 – 19 May 1720
Newport	Sloop	S-N-006	26					X		30 May 1723 – 13 Jun 1723
Newport	Sloop	S-N-007	26					X		11 Oct 1723 – 5 Dec 1723
Nightingale	Sloop	S-N-008	27		X	X				9 Jun 1720 – 18 May 1721

O

Ship Names	Type	Ship ID#	Page #	19	20	21	22	23	24	Date Range
Olive Branch	Sloop	S-O-003	76		X	X				15 Jul 1720 – 30 Nov 1721
Olive Branch	Sloop	S-O-001	27					X		4 Jul 1723 – 25 Jul 1723
Owners Goodwill	Ship	S-O-002	27					X	X	9 Dec 1723 – 7 Jan 1724

P

Ship Names	Type	Ship ID#	Page #	19	20	21	22	23	24	Date Range
Paradox	Sloop	S-P-017	73,74,75			X	X			27 Jul 1721 – 1 Nov 1722
Pennsylvania Merchant	Ship	S-P-014	38			X	X			3 Apr 1721 – 28 Aug 1722
Philadelphia	Ship	S-P-001	27		X					9 Jun 1720 – 28 Jul 1720
Philadelphia	Ship	S-P-002	27				X	X		10 May 1722 – 4 Jul 1723
Philadelphia	Sloop	S-P-003	28		X					5 May 1720 – 8 Oct 1720
Philadelphia	Sloop	S-P-004	28		X					Mar 1720 – 14 Sept 1720
Philadelphia	Schooner	S-P-005	28			X				6 Jul 1721 – 27 Jul 1721
Pearl	Sloop	S-P-016	47			X	X			12 Apr 1721 – 17 May 1722
Peggy	Sloop	S-P-006	28				X			27 Feb 1722
Pembroke	Ship	S-P-007	28				X	X		1 Nov 1722 – 18 Apr 1723
Post Boy	Sloop	S-P-015	39		X					19 May 1720 – 23 Jun 1720
Princess	Snow	S-P-008	28					X		31 Oct 1723 – 5 Dec 1723
Prince of Orange	Ship	S-P-009	29		X					26 May 1720 – 20 Dec 1720
Principio	Sloop	S-P-010	29				X			10 Mar 1722 – 15 Nov 1722
Priscilla & Merriam	Ship	S-P-011	29		X	X	X	X		18 Sept 1720 – 4 Oct 1723
Prosperity	Ship	S-P-012	29		X					14 Apr 1720
Prosperous	Sloop	S-P-013	29		X					24 Oct 1720 – 24 Nov 1720

R

Ship Names	Type	Ship ID#	Page #	19	20	21	22	23	24	Date Range
Rainbow	Sloop	S-R-001	30			X				30 May 1721 – 8 Jun 1721
Raven	Sloop	S-R-002	30					X		8 Aug 1723 – 12 Sept 1723
Rebekah	Snow	S-R-005	48	X	X					22 Dec 1719 – 7 Jul 1720
Rebekah	Sloop	S-R-009	84,85		X					7 Apr 1720 – 18 Aug 1720
"	"	"	"			X				16 Mar 1721 – 13 Apr 1721
"	"	"	"			X				28 Aug 1721 – 5 Oct 1721
"	"	"	"				X	X		26 Apr 1722 – 8 Aug 1723
Richard & Elizabeth	Sloop	S-R-008	82					X		26 Sept 1723 – 24 Oct 1723
Richard & Mary	Sloop	S-R-010	86,87			X	X			17 Jan 1721 – 5 Jul 1722
Richard & Mary	Ship	S-R-003	30					X		13 Jun 1723 – 4 Jul 1723
Richmond	Ship	S-R-006	63					X		24 Oct 1723 – 17 Dec 1723
Robert & James	Sloop	S-R-007	65,67			X	X	X		20 Apr 1721 – 29 Jul 1723
Royal George	Ship	S-R-004	30	X	X					29 Dec 1719 – 18 Jan 1720

S

Ship Names	Type	Ship ID#	Page #	19	20	21	22	23	24	Date Range
Salamander	Sloop	S-S-033	70,71,72		X	X	X			24 Nov 1720 – 6 Sept 1722
Samuel	Sloop	S-S-001	30		X					9 Jun 1720 – 7 Jul 1720
Samuel & Anne	Snow	S-S-035	77					X		26 Sept 1723 – 7 Nov 1723
Samuel & Mary	Sloop	S-S-002	30				X			29 Nov 1722 – 11 Dec 1722
Samuel & Sarah	Sloop	S-S-021	44	X	X					22 Dec 1719 – 3 Nov 1720
Sarah	Scallop	S-S-003	30					X		25 Jul 1723 – 29 Jul 1723
Sarah	Ship	S-S-020	40			X	X	X		27 Jul 1721 – 14 Nov 1723
Sarah	Sloop	S-S-025	54		X	X	X			7 Mar 1720 – 5 Jul 1722
Sarah	Sloop	S-S-019	39			X	X	X		27 Apr 1721 – 21 Nov 1723
Sarah	Sloop	S-S-022	46			X				24 Aug 1721 – 7 Dec 1721
Sarah	Brigantine	S-S-028	59		X					7 Mar 1720 – 6 Dec 1720
Sarah	Snow	S-S-029	59,60			X	X	X		17 Jan 1721 – 26 Sept 1723
Sarah	Sloop	S-S-031	67	X	X	X				22 Dec 1719 – 7 Dec 1721
Sarah	Ship	S-S-037	82,83		X	X	X			19 May 1720 – 6 Sept 1722
Sarah & Mary	Sloop	S-S-004	31		X					28 Nov 1720 – 27 Dec 1720
Sarah & Mary	Sloop	S-S-026	57				X	X	X	5 Apr 1722 – 16 Jul 1724
Sarah & Mary	Sloop	S-S-030	61				X			8 Nov 1722 – 11 Dec 1722

YEARS COVERED / 22 Dec 1719 – 7 Jan 1724

S

Ship Names	Type	Ship ID#	Page #	19	20	21	22	23	24	Date Range
Sea Flower	Sloop	S-S-027	58		X					23 Feb 1720 – 19 May 1720
Sea Flower	Sloop	S-S-005	31			X	X			9 Nov 1721 – 1 Nov 1722
Sea Nymph	Sloop	S-S-006	31			X				18 May 1721 – 21 Jun 1721
Society	Sloop	S-S-007	31			X	X			26 Oct 1721 – 10 Mar 1722
Speedwell	Sloop	S-S-008	31			X				30 Mar 1721 – 20 Apr 1721
Speedwell	Sloop	S-S-009	32			X				7 Sept 1721 – 28 Sept 1721
Speedwell	Sloop	S-S-010	32			X				28 Sept 1721 – 5 Oct 1721
Speedwell	Sloop	S-S-011	32				X			9 Aug 1722 – 6 Sept 1722
Speedwell	Sloop	S-S-012	32					X		4 Jul 1723
Sperma Caeti	Sloop	S-S-013	32			X				15 Jun 1721 – 29 Jun 1721
Starling	Ship	S-S-014	32			X				9 Nov 1721 – 30 Nov 1721
St Christopher's	Sloop	S-S-024	53					X		21 Nov 1723
St Peter	Snow	S-S-034	75		X					7 Apr 1720 – 23 Jun 1720
Susanna	Sloop	S-S-015	33		X					12 May 1720 – 19 May 1720
Susanna	Sloop	S-S-032	69		X					14 Jul 1720 – 10 Oct 1720
Susanna	Sloop	S-S-036	81		X	X				2 Feb 1720 – 7 Dec 1721
Susanna	Sloop	S-S-023	51					X		4 Apr 1723 – 9 May 1723
Susanna	Ship	S-S-018	37				X			5 Apr 1722 – 14 Jun 1722
Swallow	Schooner	S-S-016	33	X	X					18 Dec 1719 – 28 Mar 1720
"	"	"	"				X	X		16 Apr 1722 – 21 Sept 1723
Syzeragh / Sizergh	Ship	S-S-017	34					X		26 Feb 1723 – 9 May 1723

T

Ship Names	Type	Ship ID#	Page #	19	20	21	22	23	24	Date Range
Three Brothers	Sloop	S-T-007	48		X	X	X			6 Aug 1720 – 18 Oct 1722
Three Brothers	Sloop	S-T-008	49		X					28 Apr 1720 – 24 Oct 1720
Three Sisters	Sloop	S-T-009	52	X	X	X				9 Dec 1719 – 30 Nov 1721
Three Williams	Sloop	S-T-005	43			X	X			7 Aug 1721 – 15 Nov 1722
Thomas & Sarah	Sloop	S-T-001	34				X			18 Oct 1722
Traveler	Sloop	S-T-003	39		X					4 Jan 1720 – 18 Jan 1720
Trine Hope	Ship	S-T-002	34		X	X	X	X		7 Apr 1720 – 18 Sept 1723
Tryal	Schooner	S-T-006	47		X	X				13 Aug 1720 – 7 Dec 1721
Two Brothers	Sloop	S-T-004	42						X	1724

U

Ship Names	Type	Ship ID#	Page #	19	20	21	22	23	24	Date Range
Unity	Sloop	S-U-001	84,86,87	X	X	X	X			22 Dec 1719 – 29 Nov 1722

V

Ship Names	Type	Ship ID#	Page #	19	20	21	22	23	24	Date Range
Vine	Sloop	S-V-002	44		X	X				6 Oct 1720 – 7 Dec 1721
Vine	Sloop	S-V-001	43				X	X		16 Aug 1722 – 21 Nov 1723

W

Ship Names	Type	Ship ID#	Page #	19	20	21	22	23	24	Date Range
Whitehaven	Sloop	S-W-010	66					X		2 May 1723 – 24 Dec 1723
William	Sloop	S-W-009	39		X					1 Jun 1720 – 7 Oct 1720
William	Sloop	S-W-001	35		X	X	X			23 Oct 1720 – 3 Dec 1722
William	Sloop	S-W-002	35		X					14 Sept 1720 – 13 Dec 1720
William	Sloop	S-W-003	35		X					15 Sept 1720 – 13 Oct 1720
William	Sloop	S-W-004	35		X					27 Aug 1720 – 29 Sept 1720
William	Sloop	S-W-005	36			X				23 Mar 1721 – 8 Jun 1721
William	Sloop	S-W-006	36				X			26 Apr 1722 – 31 May 1722
William & Mary	Brigantine	S-W-007	36			X				Jun 1721 – 23 Nov 1721
William & Mary	Sloop	S-W-008	36		X					20 Apr 1720 – 16 Jun 1720

Source #	Title	Publisher	Year	Vol
3	*Minutes of the Provincial Council of Pennsylvania*	Jo. Severns & Co	1852	III
5	*American Weekly Mercury / 1719 – 1720*	The Colonial Society of Pennsylvania	1898	I
6	*American Weekly Mercury / 1720 – 1721*	The Colonial Society of Pennsylvania	1898	II
7	*American Weekly Mercury / 1721 – 1722*	The Colonial Society of Pennsylvania	1905	III
8	*American Weekly Mercury / 1722 – 1723*	The Colonial Society of Pennsylvania	1907	IV
20	*The New England Courant / 7 Aug 1721 – 4 Jun 1726*	James & Benjamin Franklin	1721+	ISSUES
22	*American Weekly Mercury / 1724*	Andrew Bradford	1724	ISSUES